"One of the things I've or over twenty years, is fe has on their marriage ys makes its way into mur swipe-right, hook up culture that leave people desperate for intimacy. Crystal uses her own personal experience combined with Godly wisdom to speak through the noise of dating and right to the heart. This book is a valuable resource for anyone trying to honor God as they date."

Justin Davis
Author, Beyond Ordinary: When a Good Marriage Just Isn't Good Enough
Founder, RefineUs Ministries

"Christian dating advice too often is aimed at your young 20-something in Bible college. That leaves far too many out of the equation. Dating Done Right helps those who need practical, biblical advice on dating with purpose—stripped of condescension, pat answers, and over-spiritualization."

Sheila Wray Gregoire,
Author of The Good Girl's Guide to Great Sex

"Oh how I wish I had this book twenty years ago. I found my way to Jesus in my late twenties. Traversing the tricky paths of dating after I became a Christian (or even if I should date at all) was challenging at times. This book answers so many practical questions about dating that I remember asking: What is purity culture? What is courting, and is it the only answer? And, how do I handle the waiting… the endless waiting for 'The One'? Crystal gives solid, clear, and biblical answers to all of these questions and more. I have now been married for twelve years, but I am still able to relate and apply Crystal's ideas to my own relationship with my husband. But, more importantly, I can apply the encouragement in this book to my relationship with myself. I highly recommend this book for anyone who is wondering how to do life on this planet with a longing for fruitful and honest relationships. And… aren't we all?"

Dana Bowman
Author and Speaker at MomsieBlog.com

"Dating Done Right is that conversation you should have with a great friend over coffee for months. Crystal hits the high points of dating with authenticness, wisdom and practicality. This is a great read for anyone single or dating."

Douglas Weiss Ph.D.
Exec. Dir. Heart to Heart Counseling Center

"During my single years, I always thought there was nothing worse than reading advice on singleness and dating from people who got married at 21. What did they know about what I called 'prolonged singleness?' As I aged into my late twenties and crossed into my thirties, I began to wonder if I was going to be single forever and, several times, thought of settling. Very few resources out there acknowledged the hard reality of being single when you desperately wanted to get married. This is the book I needed then. Crystal writes from a place of experience not "expertise." She speaks intentionality and truth into what can be a difficult and lonely journey of waiting and offers practical insight and questions to help move a relationship along. I (finally) got married at 33 and I can tell you that the truths and strategies laid out in this book are vital for the health of a relationship."

Jessica Harris
Author & Speaker at BeggarsDaughter.com

"Crystal has written a book that EVERYONE should read, whether you've never been married, are currently married, or have been divorced. It's not just another book for singles. It's a powerhouse of wisdom I'm so grateful I had the opportunity to read as a single woman myself still hopeful for not just marriage, but a healthy marriage. Crystal will take you on a journey of digging deeper into knowing who you truly are in Christ, which is something we all must know before we attempt to find our identities in others. The thought-provoking questions she asks in the book really opened my eyes to some things I didn't even know about myself and challenged me to continue working on my heart as I seek God in finding the man I want to do life with. A must read!"

Sundi Jo Graham
Author & Speaker at SundiJo.com

DATING DONE Right

PURSUING RELATIONSHIPS ON PURPOSE

CRYSTAL RENAUD DAY, MAPC

© 2019
BY CRYSTAL RENAUD DAY

All rights reserved. No part of this book may be reproduced in any form without permission in writing from the author, except in the case of brief quotations embodied in critical articles or reviews.

Scripture quotations marked NIV are taken from the Holy Bible, New International Version®, NIV®. Copyright ©1973, 1978, 1984 by Biblica, Inc.™ Used by permission of Zondervan. All rights reserved worldwide.

Scripture quotations marked NLT are taken from the Holy Bible, New Living Translation, copyright © 1996, 2004. Used by permission of Tyndale House Publishers, Inc., Wheaton Illinois 60189, U.S.A. All rights reserved.

All websites and phone numbers listed herein are accurate at the time of publication but may change in the future or cease to exist. The listing of website references and resources does not imply author endorsement of the site's entire contents. Groups and organizations are listed for informational purposes, and listing does not imply author endorsement of all their activities.

Edited by: Crystal Renaud Day, Jennifer Miller
Interior Design: Crystal Renaud Day
Cover Design: James Ulysse
ISBN: 9781082278815

Published by
LIVING ON PURPOSE, LLC
KANSAS CITY

To my husband Tim.

I never imagined I'd write those words
God is faithful, friends. Just wait and see.

Table of Contents

Introduction: Dating Advice from a Non-Dater   9

Section One: SINGLE

Chapter 1: Finding Purpose in the Season   17
Chapter 2: Getting Comfortable with Being Single   29
Chapter 3: Do You Know Who You Are?   41
Chapter 4: Family Matters   55
Chapter 5: You Are Allowed to Have a Past   69
    (Your Spouse Will Have One Too)

Section Two: DATING

Chapter 6: Kiss Dating Hello   83
Chapter 7: Finding Someone Worth Falling For   93
Chapter 8: The First Date   105
Chapter 9: Common Dating Pitfalls to Watch Out For   117
Chapter 10: Digging Deeper as a Couple   127

Section Three: ENGAGED

Chapter 11: The Natural Next Step   145
Chapter 12: Bibbity Bobbity Boo   157
Chapter 13: Marriage is a Choice   169

Conclusion: Just a Few Final Words   179

About the Author   185
Acknowledgements   187
Resources   189
Notes   191

Introduction:
Dating Advice from a Non-Dater

"I date... But you know, both times were totally screwed up."
Gracie Hart, Miss Congeniality

At 32 years, 7 months, and 4 days old I went on my very first date. The man I went on that date with became my husband 364 days later. You might be thinking, "Great, I just bought a book about dating from some lady who has no experience or worse, from a married lady who can't possibly relate to my life." I understand both trains of thought. I never wanted to be the kind of person who found love, got married, and started telling singles and dating couples how to live their lives as if I somehow knew best. Those people bugged me so badly when I was single. I too felt they could

---

· Bullock, S. (Producer), & Petrie, D. (Director). (2000). *Miss Congeniality* [Motion Picture].

not possibly relate or even understand my experiences as a single woman. I too felt they had all but forgotten what it was like to feel the pain of yet another night in without a date or the heartbreak of another date gone badly. I promised myself that I would not become one of those people, and yet here I am. I want you to know though that helping singles has always been an area of passion for me, in no small part to my own difficult experiences. Now that I'm married and have navigated the tricky waters of dating and falling in love, I feel even more passionate and frankly, obligated to serve the single community. I also know the ring on my finger may alienate you from me, but I pray it doesn't have to. I pray you can look past the jewelry to see my heart for you.

I met my husband Tim on June 23, 2017 on an Internet dating site. I will refrain from telling you which one; after all, they aren't paying me to advertise for them. I will say however that I had profiles on several sites over the years before I landed on this one. In fact, I sort of joined this one as a last resort. Before Tim, in all of my years of having profiles on dating websites, I only ever received a few messages from guys. Those few also included a couple of marriage proposals from some Green Card seekers. One match I received on an Internet dating site said that premarital sex was permissible if marriage was imminent. His vocation? A pastor. I am not sure what Bible he was reading, but it wasn't the same as mine.

When I met Tim, I was not optimistic about online dating anymore, especially after a recent ghosting incident (more on that later). However, after a couple of emails back and forth with him and then a couple days of chatting on the phone, the first real life date I ever went on (with Tim or otherwise) took place on June 25, 2017. I say real life date because the only other date I went on prior to this was when I was 18 years old. When a high school friend was deployed to Iraq, he asked me out on a date before he left. Truthfully, it was more of a meaningful way for two friends to say goodbye. I am happy to report that he came back home and is now happily married with kids. As I was saying, my first real date was with Tim. One year to the day he sent me that first message on a dating site, we were married. Our dating and engagement period of only a year might seem short to some. Something to understand about dating and engagements, they do not have to be long and drawn out. This is especially true for couples that go into dating one another who are on the same page.

Tim and I met, dated, fell in love with one another, and got married just like any other traditional couple. The difference here was that I was at the point in my life I intentionally went into dating with marriage in mind. I was not interested in casual dating. I had found contentment in being single so if I was going to date, I was going to date with purpose. It just so happened that Tim also went into dating with marriage in mind. As a result, when we ended up on each other's path, there were no games, mismatched motives, or unknown expectations. It was all very black and white, with very little gray area about what we were expecting. We knew what we wanted from a dating relationship and from a future spouse. I am thankful to say that we found it in each other. It is often said that when you know, you know. That is absolutely true when you do this whole dating thing right.

At the time of the publication of this book, my husband and I have been married a year and a half. It is going tremendously well, but I am not an expert on marriage. This is not a marriage book, though many of the chapters are designed to prepare you for marriage. I have no plans to write a book on marriage for a while (if at all). I do, however, have many, many years of experience being single. You could think of me as your Yoda of Singleness. That's a nod to my husband as I only just saw Star Wars (Episodes 4-6) for the first time a few months ago. I was single for almost 33 years before I met Tim and I believe I navigated that time well. I hope to share my experiences with you through the chapters to come. The older I got, the more weddings I attended and my list of single friends grew shorter and shorter. "Always a bridesmaid, never a bride" was not just a saying in my life—it was a theme. By the time I met Tim, my closest community of friends were all married with children and most of them had been married for well over a decade. However, I was blessed by how they loved me and invited me into their homes and families.

  The hard part was that they were so far removed from their past. Being single and dating was so far from their minds. When I would complain about being single, their well-meaning words were hard to listen to at times. They would tell me that God was faithful (true). They would tell me that he was out there for me. Some of them shared how old they were when they met their husbands as a way to try to say it wasn't too late for me. That helped for a while until I became older than they were when they got married. Once I broke that age barrier, those words were less and less helpful. They honestly did not know what it was like for me. While I am no longer single, I want to be the kind of friend for you that I wished I had. I want to be someone that can share relatable advice from my own recent history. I once saw a meme that said, "My entire goal in life is to show my friends who are not single how awesome being single is." That is how I tried to live my life when I was single and that is what I hope for you as well. I understand what it is like to be single and wonder if it is a chronic condition. I know that it helps to have a friend who understands where you are—right where you are.

**HELLO, MY NAME IS CRYSTAL,
AND I WANT TO BE THAT FRIEND TO YOU.**

Before I met Tim, singleness was something I had a pretty solid handle on. It was what came after being single that was really the mystery. I was inspired to write this book while Tim and I were dating because we could not find a resource that helped us navigate our dating journey well. Aside from a devotional bible for engaged couples, there weren't any resources available to help couples with the tough stuff. There was nothing that helped to navigate the conversations that make or break a relationship. There definitely weren't any that were designed for men or women and for couples to read together. Instead, we kind of had to figure it out for ourselves. I am thankful that the way Tim and I approached dating and the conversations we had before and after our engagement set us up for success. Now I can share what we learned with you.

If you have always been single, I want to encourage you to let go of any preconceived ideas. If you are single again, I want to encourage you to not allow the fear of the past to rob you of the joy of what could be next for you.

Whether you have always been single or are single again, this book has been created as a guide of sorts, based on the things Tim and I did right, but also what we did wrong. It also contains anecdotes from my personal journey and some professional advice from me as well. Can I promise you that if you follow the advice in this book that the love of your life is just around the corner?

Absolutely and irrevocably not.

I have no idea where the love of your life is (sorry, but it is true). My heart in writing this book is to get you ready for them AND to support you once you find them.

THIS BOOK IS BROKEN UP INTO THREE SECTIONS:
- SINGLE
- DATING
- ENGAGED

These sections intentionally take you on a journey from singleness, to dating, and finally to engagement because that is how a healthy relationship should naturally evolve. It might seem dubious to have a section on engagement in a book about singleness and dating, especially if you are reading this as single as can be. Dating Done Right is about dating with marriage in mind. By far the largest section is dating, but do not skip ahead. *Even if you are already dating someone.* That is because the journey begins as a single individual. It may even mean that you keep this book handy as a part of your nightstand collection for a while.

Part of being single is getting to know yourself first so then you can share who you are with another person. That takes time. Going on a first date, a second date, or even a third date does not mean you are in a relationship. Getting to that point takes time. It is not until you have a conversation to define the relationship that you are actually dating someone. Hopefully at that point you are dating each other with a mindset of marriage. Until then, you are still just one single person getting to know another single person to determine if there is enough compatibility to take it to the next level. However, that does not mean that you should be going on dates with multiple people at the same time. It also does not mean that you will become engaged to the next person you date. That takes time too. It simply means that developing a relationship is a process and it is best to start it off right.

Or as it were… *dating… done right.*

Section One:
SINGLE

Chapter 1:
Finding Purpose in the Season

"If women really wanted to change society, they could do it. I plan to change it. I just want to get married first!" Ally, Ally McBeal

    Singles are one of the most, if not *the* most, underserved demographics in the church community today. Trust me, I would know. Not long ago, I too sat alone in church services listening to sermons on marriage and family. I walked alone into bible studies and home groups with a sea of married women and married couples with their kids. I longed for a singles ministry to belong to, only to have my church not offer one. I looked up other local churches to see if they had singles ministries to join, only to find there were not any nearby. In my own church, I felt as though I had

---

· Pontell, J. (Director). (1994). I know him by heart. [Television series episode] In D. Kelley (Producer), *Ally McBeal*. Manhattan Beach, CA: 20th Century Fox Television.

to advocate for myself in order to be seen just as I am even though I was a consistent, tithing, volunteering member of the body. When it comes to people being single in the church today, not much room is created for them. Instead, they are seen as almost incomplete. Without a ring, there isn't a place to belong. Most of the time, if singles are addressed, it all comes down to sex. Singles in the church are told to wait until marriage to have sex. In some churches, singles might also be told that it is better to be courted than to date. They might also be told to be careful putting themselves in positions that could lead to sex, such as being alone with the opposite sex. Women are told to dress modestly to avoid being tempting. Men are told to bounce their eyes to avoid being tempted. For many, this conversation was given as part of the purity culture movement.

Purity culture essentially said that if you have sex before marriage or live with a boyfriend or girlfriend before marriage, you are a big, fat sinner. Purity culture left no room for grace or redemption. I am not saying that sex before marriage is right or good. One glaring omission from the purity culture conversation however, is why wait to have sex until marriage. Purity culture was well intentioned, but left many evangelical singles to have unhealthy relationships with religion, dating, marriage, and of course sex. Sex became shameful, instead of being God's greatest gift to share within marriage. Perhaps you have experienced something similar.

After youth group, singleness and dating is almost never brought up again, especially not from the pulpit. While no longer discussed specifically, the expectation from purity culture is deeply ingrained. There is also a tremendous amount of judgment placed on unmarried, cohabiting couples that visit churches, not to mention the judgment placed on single parents and divorced singles. It doesn't seem to matter that singles are regularly witnessing sexual sin by married members. Instead of church leaders addressing the adultery, porn addiction, and swinging happening right under their noses, singles are the ones perceived as the problem children. When I was single, I personally experienced married women in the church seeing my singleness as a threat to their marriages. I once overheard a card carrying, ordained pastor talk about why he did not support singles ministries. His reasoning was that he felt they all become nothing more than a meat market that inevitably turns into a hook up spot. Basically, his reason came down to singles are sex-crazed fiends who don't deserve a community to grow in their faith with others of their same life stage. What does it say to singles when their own church sees them this way and not as valuable members of the body? If that is really how singles are perceived, is it any wonder why they are leaving the church altogether? Is it any wonder why Christian singles are becoming exactly what they have been told they are? To me, it says a lot more about the leaders who run singles ministries (or don't offer singles ministries at all) than it does the singles that attend them. I could write a whole other book about the church's responsibility to singles, but I will move on.

  If we are being honest, it is not just the church that is doing a disservice to singles today. Singles are also grossly underserved by the mainstream culture. If you take your dating advice from the mainstream culture, you are encouraged to make compromises and settle for less than God's best for your life. Saving oneself for marriage is often seen as a punch line in movies and television. Instead, singles are encouraged to sleep around, watch porn, or masturbate because it is all perceived as normal, healthy sexual exploration and expression. As a result, singles wind up hurt and even lonelier than when they started out. Or worse, they settle for marrying the wrong person at the wrong time. Perhaps you know exactly what I am talking about because you have experienced that for yourself.

By the way singles are dismissed and misguided, one could say singles are the most underserved demographic in the country today. If these are the only two extremely polarized options (purity church culture vs. secular culture) offered to singles today, where do good, God-loving singles turn to for dating advice? My hope is that you can turn to this book ... but ultimately my hope is that you turn to the One who created sex, love, and marriage in the first place. Doing so, you just might discover that purity culture was just as against God's design for sex, love, and marriage as secular culture is today.

THE SURVEY SAYS...

As I began writing this book, I designed a survey for singles to share their experiences with me. Questions asked were related to dating, church culture, purity culture, mainstream culture, and even living single among a world of well-meaning married couples. 124 men and women completed the survey. I want to share some of the results of that survey with you in this book for a couple of reasons: 1) so you do not feel so alone in your frustrations and 2) to shine a light on the experiences of singles today:

SURVEY QUESTIONS & RESULTS

HOW OLD WERE YOU WHEN YOU FIRST STARTED DATING?
- 16% were between 13-15 years old
- 20% were between 16-19 years old
- 24% were between 20-25 years old
- 8% were between 26-30 years
- 5% were between 31-35 years old
- 1% were between 36-40 years old

NEVER BEEN KISSED
26% of those surveyed said that had never even been on a date—the highest % of all. While it might seem like everyone paired off in high school and college, it is just not true. I have personally known women other than myself who entered into their 30's still waiting for their first date, their first kiss, and their first love. Some of them are still waiting. **If that is you, you are not alone!**

HOW LONG WAS YOUR LONGEST DATING RELATIONSHIP?
- 10% less than one month
- 24% less than six months
- 11% less than one year
- 15% less than 18 months
- 13% more than two years

WHEN WAS THE LAST TIME YOU WENT ON A DATE?
- 13% less than one week ago
- 10% less than one month ago
- 12% less than six months ago
- 7% less than one year ago
- 32% of those surveyed haven't been on a date in over a year!

As you can see from the survey results, the surprising theme is how few people are actively dating. There is a misconception that singles are out there serial dating, jumping from one relationship to the next. The truth is, Christian singles today are choosing to abstain from dating altogether. One of the main reasons for this, in my opinion, is a lack of places to meet potential dates. **To me, the saddest result of the survey was in response to the question,** *"Does your church have a ministry/program for single adults?"* **Out of the 124 survey takers, 76 of them indicated that the church they attend did not have a singles ministry. Out of those 76, 52 of them said they would attend one if their church offered it.** Too many churches are not offering a way for their singles to meet—leaving them to fend for themselves with things like social media, online dating, and everything in between in an attempt to meet.[1] Swiping left is just not going to do it. Without events at church, the idea of Christian singles meeting organically today is all but lost.

In the survey, I also asked questions where the surveyor was able to give a written response. The first one was, *"What do you think of when you hear the word courtship?"* Based solely on the survey, you would think that *courting* was an extremely profane word. Surveyors had strong feelings about it—mostly negative. For example, one surveyor wrote, "Strict Christian conservativism, not in touch with reality. Stupid... too much pressure." Another said, "Old-fashioned, strict, and unrealistic expectations." One surveyor simply put, "Errr no." I will unpack courting more, including the real meaning of it in a later chapter. I also asked, *"What do you think of when you hear the word submission?"* As you can imagine, the responses to that question were also negative. For example, one surveyor wrote, "It means making yourself lower than the other person, letting them be the boss even when you don't want to."

Another wrote, "Me losing my brain, dreams, opinions to someone I blindly have to accept as my spiritual head." Ouch. I will also unpack submission in a later chapter, but I will give you a hint: that's not what submission means at all.

SINGLE ON PURPOSE

Now that you know what inspired me to write this book, we can begin to dig into your own story. One thing I discovered when I was seeking some endorsements is how few Christian leaders (i.e. pastors, worship leaders, speakers, authors, etc.) are single. When I was single and started my first nonprofit ministry, I battled finding my own voice among Christian leaders. I could feel the tension of being female *and* single in Christian leadership circles. I thought it was *only* because I was a single, Christian *woman*, but the more I looked, there aren't many single *men* leading either. I feel like there is something to be learned from this. There are two questions that come to mind in response to this observation: Are there no single leaders because their marital status somehow qualifies them? Or are there no single leaders because they are waiting on marriage to get started? It is quite possible that both of those questions are true.

One of the first (and only) things I ever wrote on singleness before now was a blog post entitled, *"Single on Purpose."* It would later become a speaking topic I so loved to present on the student ministry level. Too often, those who are single choose not pursue their calling. Instead, they wait around hoping that marriage will come. When I say *calling*, I don't necessarily mean a vocational call to ministry unless that's your thing. I mean your God-given purpose—what you have been set apart by God to do with your life. For some, there's this belief that they won't be able to discover that until marriage. As a result, they sort of sit in the waiting room for their life to get started. It is not just women who do this though.

There are misconceptions (maybe) that while you are still single, you can't fully realize your God-given purpose in life. Unfortunately, this is also often pushed on singles from those who do not see them as ready to lead. Others often see singles as lacking the proper life experience to influence others. I personally struggled with this tension before I got married, both while I was on staff at a church and after I became a life coach. Many married individuals struggle with accepting advice, leadership, wisdom, what have you, from single people—as if being single means they missed the train somewhere along the way. However, one should consider Paul from scripture:

Paul was set apart to do great things for the Lord. After years of killing Christians as a Pharisee, he converted to Christianity and became one of the most influential Christian missionaries to ever walk the earth. He planted many churches and personally discipled many men and women. He is also attributed to authoring as many as 13 books of the New Testament including 1 & 2 Corinthians, 1 & 2 Timothy, Romans, Ephesians, and Galatians. He did all of this as a single man, who from what we know of scripture, never married. You could say his marital status doesn't matter, but it really does. Paul had this to say about being single:

"I want you to be free from the concerns of this life. An unmarried man can spend his time doing the Lord's work and thinking how to please him. But a married man has to think about his earthly responsibilities and how to please his wife. His interests are divided. In the same way, a woman who is no longer married or has never been married can be devoted to the Lord and holy in body and in spirit. But a married woman has to think about her earthly responsibilities and how to please her husband. I am saying this for your benefit, not to place restrictions on you. I want you to do

whatever will help you serve the Lord best, with as few distractions as possible." 1 Corinthians 7:32-35 NLT

What if you could begin to see your singleness as an opportunity? What if you could begin to see your singleness as God setting you apart to fulfill your purpose now? If you could begin to see your singleness this way, you would be amazed at how much more content you will find yourself in this season of your life. **Hear me when I say that there is nothing wrong with desiring to be married and have a family.** This book is created to help you prepare for both. However, this time of singleness can be an opportunity for you to be totally about the Lord's work both in your own life and in the lives of others.

You could even take my story as an example. I did not live my life when I was single as if marriage was even an option. I worked for a church for seven years. I started a non-profit ministry (the first of its kind). I went on four short-term missions trips. I published my first book at the age of 26. I went back to school at the age of 27. I met Tim while I was still in grad school and I didn't quit when I got my 'MRS' degree. Had I met Tim ten or even five years ago, I would not have had even half of the experiences I have had as an adult. I do not regret a moment of it. As we enter into these next few chapters on singleness, reflect on what it would mean for you to be single on purpose because as of this moment, you are.

FINDING PURPOSE QUESTIONS

When was the last time you went on a date?
If you don't date, why not?

True date — never
never been shown what a true lady should be shown

How do you typically meet new people, including friends?

Church work Stores
very social

What does your community of friends look like? Mostly single? Mostly married? Mix of both?

Divorced or single
work — young + married

As a single person, do you feel embraced by your community of friends?

Yes

Do you attend church regularly and/or participate in a group Bible study? If not, why?

Yes

As a single person, do you feel embraced by your church?

Yes

In what ways have you been sitting in the waiting room?

Waiting to live really

Have you considered what your God-given purpose for this life is?

Yes to be like Him + to show love + grace

What is keeping you from embracing your purpose?

Nothing

What would it look like to begin pursuing your purpose today?

Living Free + in the Fullness of life!

How would getting married impact your purpose?

don't see at this point that it would be good

Chapter 2:
Getting Comfortable with Being Single

"I'm hopeless and awkward and desperate for love!"
Chandler Bing, Friends

    A few years ago, at the age of 31, my 90-year-old grandpa asked me if I had a boyfriend. When I said no, he replied, *"You must not be looking hard enough."* I joked that he was worse than a pushy old church lady. Honestly, this is a common question *and* response from well-meaning people—perhaps it can even be considered a compliment. The problem with this response, however, is how frustrating it is to basically be told that I was doing something wrong. Other well-meaning people would say to me that I should

---

· Zuckerman, S. (Director). (1996). The one with metaphorical tunnel. [Television series episode] In Bright, Kauffman, & Crane (Producer), *Friends*. Burbank, CA: Warner Bros Television.

use my time as a single woman to work on myself. This was as if to say that when I was ready, I would find a husband. Or worse, when I was ready, God would bless me with a husband. I could not help but think upon hearing this advice that they were saying there was something wrong with me. When a single person is told by a married person that if they work on themselves, God will bring their spouse, it tells them that he or she is not good enough just as they are. What did I need to work on that would all of a sudden make me dateable or marriable? What did I need to work on in order for God to see me as worthy of marriage?

Even if that is not the intent of the advice, it is how it is heard. I would look around at the people I knew close to my age who had already married and thought, "How were they more ready than me?" There are a lot, and I mean a lot of people who are married today who were not ready to walk down the aisle when they did. I fought the notion that maybe I'd be married had I just worked on myself sooner. The truth is, both sets of advice are wrong. No amount of looking hard would have revealed a husband to me sooner. No amount of self-improvement would have attracted a husband to me sooner.

I do not believe in coincidences. If I were supposed to be married five, ten, or even fifteen years ago, I would have been. If you were supposed to be married by now, you would be. **Jesus was single, by the way, and no one ever accused Him of being less than whole.** Being married does not make you whole because you are whole just as you are. Trusting in God's timing about the when and the how takes the pressure off of you. Instead, it gives the control of your future all back into God's hands where it belongs. That is not to say there weren't areas of my life that could use some improvement. The same is true of you. There is always the need to work on oneself as God continues to pursue us through the process of sanctification. In the time between you being single and married, you do have a unique opportunity to work on some things. Perhaps, most importantly, getting comfortable with being single in the first place.

If you bought this book because you are desperate to get married or thought it would give you some quick tips on finding the love of your life, you may be sorely disappointed. While I am a certified life coach (and even a masters level pastoral counselor now), finding the love of your life is not the point of this book. However, I hope you keep reading. There is no formula for meeting someone, falling in love with them, and living happily ever after together. There is no potion or elixir to drink either. I wrote this book to help singles to get comfortable with being single above all else. Truthfully, if you are not comfortable in your own skin right where you are as a single individual, then you will never be comfortable in a relationship (i.e. dating, married, or otherwise). There is a saying that goes, *"wherever you go, there you are."* That statement is never truer than when someone is in a relationship.

Dating and marriage is not about being with someone to help you feel less alone. You can alleviate some aspects of loneliness by renting a room out to a friend or joining a bowling league. I say some aspects because some of the loneliest times I have felt in my life, I was surrounded by people. The issue was not that I did not have people around me who loved and cared for me. The problem was, I did not have enough love and care for myself. I had the idea in my head that if I had a boyfriend or a husband, I would be happy and feel fulfilled. I had to learn to be content and become fulfilled on my own. The truth is, it is okay to be alone. It is even okay to be lonely at times. You must learn to be comfortable being *by* yourself in order to be comfortable *being* yourself in a relationship. Have you considered what being married means? Unless you plan to live in a different house from your spouse (which to me does not sound ideal for a number of reasons), marriage means someone lives with you. Marriage means someone is going to load the dishwasher wrong sometimes. Marriage means that somehow the one or two loads of laundry you do per week now becomes six or seven. Marriage means making physical space in the home for each other. Marriage means making emotional and mental space for each other. Marriage means being vulnerable—no pretext. All of those things are helped a great deal if you like the person you marry, and it helps if the person you marry likes you too. If you take the time to get to know yourself and even come to like yourself, the person you date and one day marry will learn to know the *real* you too—not a well contrived version of you.

DATING YOURSELF + Jesus

The purpose for the entire SINGLE section of this book is to take a step back from thinking about finding a spouse but in a sense, finding you instead. Dating Done Right begins with dating yourself first. Dating yourself before you date someone else is critical because you are not going to find yourself in someone else. You cannot begin to share with someone else who you are if you are unsure of that yourself. Dating yourself is exactly what it sounds like. It is about you getting to know you: what you like, what you don't like, discovering what is holding you back from being your authentic self, explore what you want for your future, and even fall in love with yourself—perhaps for the first time in your life. There is a large correlation between how you feel about yourself and how you allow yourself to be treated. There's an equal or greater correlation between how you feel about yourself and what you think you deserve. How you allow yourself to be treated and what you think you deserve both play a major role in the type of person you may very well end up marrying. If you struggle with self worth or believe you do not deserve good things, you are more likely to attract individuals who will further exacerbate those feelings in you. Loving yourself makes you loveable in the way you deserve first, and also how you should be loved by someone else.

If you believe that marriage will complete you, I am sorry to say that math doesn't add up. Marriage alone will never complete you, especially if you see yourself as incomplete just as you are today. An incomplete person marrying another incomplete person results in two incomplete people trying like mad to make it work—and likely failing to do so. When I say incomplete, I do not mean imperfect. Everyone is imperfect. I am talking about completeness in the sense of knowing yourself, knowing what you want, being healed from the wounds of the past, and being whole in Christ. Ideally, marriage should be about two complete individuals coming together in unity. **Marriage is 100% + 100%, not 50% + 50%.** Marrying the right person will shore up your weaknesses, of course, but you're more likely to marry the wrong person if you see marriage as a way to fix yourself or your problems. If that is your mentality, it will be a struggle for you and your partner to overcome the disappointment of discovering it doesn't work that way. We are made complete individually when we surrender our hearts and minds to Christ and heal the wounds of our past—letting go of unforgiveness, bitterness, and insecurity.

No matter how much one might try to deny it, the story of your past impacts you and makes up a large part of who you have become today. There is a pattern seen by those in mental health professions that has proven true for a lot of my own clients and even those I know personally. The pattern suggests that individuals in their 20's are prone to running away from their childhood or adolescent problems in hopes of escaping it. Then, by their 30's, their 'chickens come home to roost' so to speak as they start to experience the repercussions of running from their wounds and not healing them. These repercussions can include depression, anxiety, addiction, or other emotional health issues that negatively impact their life. Finally, by the time they hit their 40's, they become wise enough to get some help, or that is the hope at least. It is likely that if someone has not worked through their issues by then, they never will. This is not because they can't heal after 40, but there is a complacency that takes over—wounds become a crutch to stand on. No matter what lies in your past, no matter how messy or clean, everyone can benefit from counseling.

Counseling is not a bad word and the sooner we can break the stigma around counseling, the better off the world will be. Unfortunately, it is among some Christian communities that counseling is the most taboo. There is a deeply held belief by many that everything that ails a person emotionally or mentally can be prayed away. If you broke your leg or your wrist, would you pray for it to be healed or would you go to the hospital for surgery and a cast? I absolutely believe in the power of prayer, however, we are also created to be in community. Community means accepting help every once in a while. A part of being in community is relying on others to help us and at times, we have to advocate for ourselves to get the kind of help we need. Consider John 5:1-7:

> "Jesus returned to Jerusalem for one of the Jewish holy days. Inside the city, near the Sheep Gate, was the pool of Bethesda, with five covered porches. Crowds of sick people—blind, lame, or paralyzed—lay on the porches. One of the men lying there had

been sick for thirty-eight years. When Jesus saw him and knew he had been ill for a long time, he asked him, 'Would you like to get well?' 'I can't, sir,' the sick man said, 'for I have no one to put me into the pool when the water bubbles up. Someone else always gets there ahead of me.' (NLT)

The man at the healing pool wasn't comfortable with being unwell, but he had grown complacent and familiar with it. There is a huge difference between being comfortable and just having a feeling of familiarity. Like this man, we too can make excuses for why we stay where we are. Things happen in life that shape us—some we can control and others we cannot. Some of those things are damaging. They can leave behind unresolved hurt, sorrow, and a deep emptiness. Counseling provides guidance and assistance in resolving these types of issues by dealing with your past in relative safety of the present. I am personally trained in both psychology and theology. My training has taught me to marry psychology and theology together to help individuals heal not just spiritually, but emotionally, and mentally as well. There is nothing taboo or wrong with counseling. Counseling should be embraced, not rejected. Let me encourage you to seek counseling if there are any indications that your motive for being in a relationship is to fix an issue within yourself. It will not go away simply by having a person on your arm.

LOVING YOURSELF

Dating yourself leads nicely into this idea of loving yourself. After all, you typically need to date someone before you fall in love with them. I have always been a little overconfident. I can look back at my middle school and high school years to see a girl who really had no reason to be confident. I was short and overweight, with braces, uncontrollable curly hair, and glasses. Yet, I had a confidence that went beyond all that. I wasn't popular in school by any means, but I had things I was good at doing and found my people. I grew up in a household where opinions were strong. I wasn't always allowed to express mine there, but outside the home I could and I most certainly did. My ability to assert myself socially aided in my ability to be confident in who I was and what I wanted. This confidence led to an ability to find things about myself that I loved. It was a proven truth that confidence and love of self comes from the inside of a person, not from what is on the outside. It might be the whole 'don't judge a book by its cover' thing. There are times where I criticize myself too harshly and doubt my abilities—that is obviously normal. Where it gets messy is when the self-criticism drowns out the self-esteem.

Look at my husband Tim. While Tim knows himself extremely well, he never learned to love himself very well. In fact, some of the best things about him are his biggest insecurities. At times I have to advocate for him because he is uncomfortable advocating for himself and what he wants. Tim's insecurities have at times been a difficult aspect of our relationship, especially early on. While I too struggled with believing someone could love me, Tim's insecurity about it was truly hard to shake. When you don't love yourself, allowing someone else to love you back is extremely difficult. At the same time however, my loving him well and sticking around to do so has broken down his walls. Tim may not fight for himself in all areas, but he fiercely fights for me. He knows how to love deeply so the capacity to love himself is there. Learning to love yourself, if you don't already, is not a skill you will become proficient in overnight.

TO AID IN THIS JOURNEY, HERE ARE A FEW WAYS TO BEGIN TO LOVE WHO YOU ARE UNCONDITIONALLY:

1. Heal your view of God and self by meditating on scriptures that describe His love for you and how He sees you. When your identity is firmly set in Him and not on the events and circumstances of your past or present, you will begin to see yourself in the way He sees you and begin to love yourself the way He loves you.
2. Grow more intimately with God through prayer.
3. Deal with the wounds of your past (i.e. counseling!)
4. Forgive others and especially yourself.
5. Spend some time alone with yourself.
6. Create and maintain healthy relational boundaries by first learning to say no to unsafe people who do not respect your boundaries.
7. Create and maintain relationships with safe people who respect your boundaries and will help you feel loved and appreciated.
8. Love others the way you would like (and deserve) to be loved.

As you work on these steps toward loving yourself, it is important to be kind to yourself in the process. There is no harsher critic of you than, well, you. The unfortunate part about this is that the enemy loves to exploit those insecurities for his own gain. This is done by feeding you lies about who you really are. As you learn to love yourself, learn to distinguish the voice of God from the voice of the enemy. Here's a hint: the voice of God does not sound like shame. There is no condemnation in Christ!

GETTING COMFORTABLE QUESTIONS

Have you experienced abuse of any kind in your past? If so, how is it impacting your life today?

Yes - afraid to be trusting of a man

Are you harboring any unforgiveness or bitterness in your heart toward anyone? If so, how is it impacting your life today?

*Probably * Asking God to show me*

Do you actively use pornography or compulsively masturbate? If so, how are these behaviors impacting your life today? (I dig deeper on this topic in Chapter 4)

*Broke this several months * Renounced * ago*

Is there anything you have done in the past that you haven't yet forgiven yourself for? If so, why are you withholding forgiveness?

Not being more mature as a Christian

Have you ever been to counseling to work on any of the issues mentioned in these questions? If so, was it helpful? Why did you stop going? If not, what has been holding you back from going?

Yes

Can you name five traits you like about yourself?

Generous   Helpful
Active   Kind

How would a friend honestly describe you to someone else?

Generous

How do you see God at this point in your life?

As my Father in Heaven who loves me as a beloved daughter

Is how you see God now different than how you saw Him in your past? If so, who or what has really changed?

Yes, perspective changed when I got divorced

How do you believe God sees you?

Passionately loves me

What has caused you to believe this way?

Reading His word & feeling His Love.

Chapter 3:
Do You Know Who You Are?

"You're so lost you don't even know what kind of eggs you like!"
Ike Graham, Runaway Bride[*]

If you have ever seen the movie *Runaway Bride* starring Julia Roberts and Richard Gere, then you may remember one specific breakfast scene. Julia Roberts' character Maggie is ordering breakfast along with her fiancé Bob. Bob orders the garden omelette with egg whites only and Maggie says it sounds good and she'll have the same. Richard Gere's character Ike overhears Maggie's order and simply says, "of course." Later, he confronts her saying that she doesn't have a mind of her own. He says she's so lost she doesn't even know what kind of eggs she likes. Little did she know,

---

[*] Field, T., Rosenberg, T., Kroopf, S., Nehra, M., & Cort, R. (Producers), & Marshall, G. (Director). (1999). *Runaway Bride* [Motion Picture].

Ike had interviewed the other men Maggie had previously left at the altar—the theme of the movie. He asked them what kind of eggs they remember Maggie liking when they were together and they all said she liked her eggs the same way as them. Since she always ate her eggs the same way as whoever she was dating, she had no idea how she actually liked her eggs. This was the catalyst to her realizing that she didn't really know herself and why she always backed out of her weddings at the last minute. It was time for her to figure out what she really wanted in her life. Later in the film, we see her trying an assortment of eggs until she decided for herself that she liked eggs benedict the best. While this an overly simplified example, the idea here is to illustrate just how easy it is to allow someone else to determine what makes you happy.

Newsflash, it is actually not the responsibility of another person (boyfriend, girlfriend, spouse, kids, etc.) to make you happy. Happiness is one of the most fluid emotions there is. That is because what makes you happy right now may not make you happy in the same way later. In fact, I can almost guarantee you of that. The kind of eggs you like may seem inconsequential. The point that I am trying to make is that it is too easy to lose yourself in the person you are dating. If you go into a relationship not having a clue about who you are, what you like, or do not like, you could become someone else entirely. The risk of doing so is six months, five years, or worse, twenty years down the road, you could wake up one morning resenting the life that was created for you in your marriage. All because you were not true to yourself at the beginning.

The flip side of the coin is the possibility of knowing yourself so well that you forget you will one day need to make room for someone else. When I got to my 30's, still single and believing I would be single forever, I feared that I had grown far too set in my ways for marriage to work. I feared that if I ever did meet a man, that I would chew him up and spit him out before the check came on the first date. I will discuss this side of the coin more in the DATING section, so fear not!

LET THE DATE BEGIN

As for this chapter, this is when dating yourself really gets going with a series of self-evaluation questions to help you get to know yourself better. The first set of self-evaluation questions are similar to the questions that you could (or should) ask on a first date (and the later chapters will elaborate on that). These are questions related to general likes and dislikes. The second set of self-evaluation questions dig a little deeper. These are the kinds of questions you should ask when you have been dating someone for a little while in order to help evaluate whether to continue the relationship. While you aren't dating yourself to discover if you should stick around with yourself, you need to know how you feel about these deeper questions.

Why am I having you do this self-evaluation now when many of these are just questions you will be answering later in a dating relationship? Well, the answer is simple: many people cannot answer the simplest of personal questions because they have never really been asked or given it much thought. Others may have grown up in an environment where their opinion was not heard or valued. As a result, forming an opinion of their own does not come naturally. A more passive individual is more likely to answer questions about themselves based on the expectations placed on them. They might also answer based on how they think the other person would answer it. An individual more desperate to be in a relationship may too easily go with someone else's opinion instead of their own in order for that person to like them more. It is also a way to avoid conflict should your thoughts, feelings, and opinions differ. How you feel, what you believe, and what you do or do not like matters. All of those things will most certainly matter to the *right* person as well, so don't lose yourself by going along with the *wrong* one!

As you begin these questionnaires, you will notice the questions are asked in such a way that does not allow for ambiguity. Meaning, they are not easily answered with a simple yes or no answer. Instead, you will need to think about your response. They are also asked in such a way that leaves little room for expectations or interpretations. This is on purpose! Each question is designed to force (I prefer to use the word encourage) you to get honest, dig deep, and really get to know yourself. At the same time, this should be fun. Since this is about dating yourself, consider going over these questions with yourself in a space you find comfortable, safe, and enjoyable. You are also encouraged to use a journal to track your responses to give yourself more space to reflect.

So go ahead, kick your feet up, and let's begin.

GETTING TO KNOW YOURSELF QUESTIONNAIRE (LIKES AND DISLIKES)

All of Your Personal Favorites

What is your favorite movie genre?

Comedy

What is your favorite music genre?

Worship then hip hop 90's :)

What is your favorite television show?

Series * The Chosen

What is your favorite book?

Redeeming Love

What is your favorite song?

always changing...

Who is your favorite musician?

Prince & Brandon Lake + Phil Wickham

Who is your favorite actor?

Andrew Ripp

What is your favorite store?

Walmart   Mardels   Kohls

What is your favorite drink?

Alani Nu / Tea * unsweet

What is your favorite snack?

unhealthy - Dots Pretzels   Healthy PB & celery

What is your favorite meal of the day?

Lunch

What was your favorite meal of all time? *(I love this question because it makes me think about a shrimp dish I had several years ago in New Orleans that I still crave!)*

Homemade Pizza

45

What is your favorite dessert?
cheese cake

What is your favorite color?
green - light + pink/coral

What is your favorite smell?
clean

What is your favorite flower?
all

What is your favorite season?
spring

What was your favorite subject in school?
Math & Accounting

Reflections on Your Personal Life

What do you do to relax?
read in recliner

What do you do for fun?
Play pickleball - Dance

What makes you laugh?
So much humor (jokes)

What makes you cry?
Everything - Jesus moving in me / His power

What was the last book you read?
Boundaries

If you have a day to yourself, how would you spend it?
Exercising reading napping

What really and truly grosses you out?
Dirty (lake) water/Slimy green

What are some of your biggest pet peeves?
inside out clothes + hair

What allergies do you have?
?? eczema

What is one thing you cannot live without?

Jesus & air

Have you ever broken a bone or surgery?

C-Sections & Hystreectomy

Reflections on Your Educational & Professional Life

What was your high school mascot?

Wagon - trailblazers

What was your first job?

Tele check

Where did you go to college?

JCCC

What did you major in or study while in college?

Accounting

What do you do for a living now?

Accounting

What do you enjoy most about your job?

The people & the grace & worth Im shown.

What do you enjoy least about your job?

Zoom meetings

What do you see yourself doing ten years from now?

? Hard to know. Into future just Good w/ God

What are the achievements in your life you are most proud of?

My children & Being single & happy

Are you an extrovert or an introvert? *(Meaning, are you energized by people—extrovert, or are you drained by people—introvert)*

extrovert more now

And of course… how do you like your eggs?

scrambled w/ cheese & butter

DIGGING DEEPER

The next set of questions dig deeper into your personal wants, values, and even beliefs about some of the most polarizing of issues. Some are more polarizing than others. These are usually social, political, and/or religious issues. The reason to ask yourself these questions is that it is not enough to simply say you believe a certain way, but to also make sure you know why you believe the way you do. It is important to know where you stand on these deeper issues so you can defend your stance and not be swayed when faced with a date with opposing views.

When these deeper questions are asked in later chapters when you are in a dating relationship, they are the kinds of questions that may make or break the decision to keep dating someone. They may be the difference between staying together and getting engaged. Some differences between yourself and the person you are dating can be good. While there are many areas with room to compromise on with a potential spouse, there are just as many that you may never budge on. Ultimately, you will have to decide for yourself where your lines in the sand are. You will also have to decide for yourself whether any of these are areas where you are willing to compromise on without compromising your values. That is why you work through questions like these now.

GETTING TO KNOW YOURSELF QUESTIONNAIRE (WANTS, VALUES, BELIEFS)

Beliefs on Faith & Social Issues

If you have a relationship with Jesus, how would you describe your faith to someone else?

Exploding, deep, intimate, proud of

Is it important to you that you and your future spouse share your same religious views? Why?

Absolutely ☆ must love Jesus w/ all our ♡'s ☆

What is your belief about alcohol consumption? Why?

no point in it for me really.

What is your belief about interracial or intercultural dating? Why?

no problem

What is your belief about gay marriage? Why?

not of God

What is your belief about abortion? Why?

not of God but wouldn't judge or condemn

What is your belief about traditional gender roles? Why?

mostly good

What is your belief about divorce? Why?

Not good since I've been divorced 2x now :-)

What is your belief about mental health counseling? Why?

Very needed

What is your belief about treating mental health disorders with medication? Why?

Not sure really

What is your belief about gambling?

Not to

What is your relationship with money?

Not healthy spend too much

How would you classify your political affiliation?

Confused

Who did you vote for in the last presidential election? Why?

Layla :-)

Do you want to have kids? Did
If you already have kids, do you want to have more?

Nope

What is your belief about birth control?

it's all good

Would you ever consider adoption to have a child? Why?

Sure

Would you ever consider fostering children in your home? Why?

Not sure

Emotional Intelligence and Self-Reflection

Do you believe in or have any regrets? Why?

Many, immature not self controlled, lust driven

What motivates you to get up each morning?

Serve God, learn more, see people

What inspires you?

People who triumph after tragedy — losing weight + being stronger

What are you most grateful for in your life?

My health & my love for Jesus

What do you worry too much about?

Future alone

What are your biggest fears?

Water (swim)

When was the last time you did something that scared you?

Shooting lessons

What kinds of things make you happy?

activity - people

When was the last time you cried?

Last night

Is your current social circle influencing you positively or negatively? How so?

Positive

Who is your best friend? Why?

Jesus   Layla
Rebecca

When was the last time you felt envious? Why?

What do you still need to forgive yourself for?

Ending up w/ Delton
& settling for so long
& losing myself

Who do you still need to forgive?

not sure

What are you holding on to that you need to let go of?

what "ifs" I would have been more mature & not ended up w/ Delton

Can you be alone without feeling lonely? If not, why?

Yes

Where in your life are you settling for less than you want?

Debt

What bad habits do you need to stop?

spending more than I earn

What good habits do you need to start?

meditation - stillness Quietness

How well do you manage the mundane?

so so

What is one thing you love the most about yourself?

polished nails / tattoos

What boundaries have you established in your life?

many since I've been seeking a whole soul.

What have you learned about yourself in the last year?

I'm stronger (physically) than I thought. I need Jesus desprately

What part of yourself are you currently working on?

my ♡
my health

What do you think is the point of being in a relationship?

Serve & Seek God

Are you putting any parts of your life on hold? Why?

relationship
& intimate

What do you spend the most time thinking about?

Yikes   being "rejected"
   feelings of abandmnt

What qualities do you admire in others?

over coming / strenght

Where do you see yourself in the next five years?

Flourishing
Healthy
Full of loving real
relationships

Chapter 4:
Family Matters

"My family is big and loud, but they're my family. We fight and we laugh, and yes, we roast lamb on a spit in the front yard. And wherever I go, whatever I do, they will always be there."
Toula Portokalos, *My Big Fat Greek Wedding*[*]

Of all of the chapters in this book, this is one feels the hardest to write. Any time the subject of family comes up, you run the risk of unintentionally hurting someone close to you. Part of getting to know yourself, however, is learning how your family has helped to shape the person you have become. For me, it feels incredibly personal to talk about how my family shaped me for

---

[*] Goetzman, G., Hanks, T., & Wilson, R. (Producers), & Zwick, J. (Director). (2002). *My Big Fat Greek Wedding* [Motion Picture].

adulthood as well as marriage—particularly my parents and their own marriage. Our families of origin have a lasting impact on us whether that impact is positive or negative. My goal for writing this chapter is not to air my family's dirty laundry. Rather, it is to get you thinking about your own family. My hope is that you discover more about how you tick, about what you may need to face, and hopefully, what you are able to learn from your experiences.

When I was growing up, my dad's career required weekly travel, and he was only ever home on the weekends. I wrote about the absence my dad's job caused and the emotional impact it had on me as a child in my first book, *Dirty Girls Come Clean*. The short story is, I didn't have a close relationship with him growing up. As I longed for one, unfortunately I looked for a replacement in negative ways. I do believe he tried the best he could or knew how. One of the ways he tried to stay connected was talking to us on the phone every night. This was the age before FaceTime or even Skype. It was hard feeling connected to him simply talking on the phone, especially when he would be calling with a short window of time. It seemed the time my dad was most present was when we were in trouble. He laid down the discipline more than my mom even though she was the one who was home. Feeling like someone is only present when you're being disciplined created a lot of resentment. Unfortunately, that was the reality for us and in some ways we are all still reaping the effects of it today. I am thankful that as an adult, I can point to good memories with my dad and I hope to create more. However, the way I grew up did cloud my view of men (and God) early on.

The dynamics that Tim grew up in aren't really mine to share. Honestly, I am still learning about them in these early years of marriage. While we were dating, we did discover we had some things in common. We had different experiences, but we were both third born. Believe it or not, birth order does play a role in the development of personality as well as parental treatment. Every child in a family has different emotional experiences growing up. I can talk to my brothers about something that happened growing up and discover that we experienced it quite differently. I was the third born, the youngest, and the only girl. Tim on the other hand was the third born, youngest boy, but also has a younger sister. Tim was both the baby in the sense he was the youngest boy, but also a middle child. Kind of interesting! In some ways, being the youngest and the only girl actually provides me with some of the traits of an only child: mature for my age, perfectionist, and a leader. Instead of me looking to my older siblings for leadership and stability, it was always I who was looked to. With my dad traveling, I began to take on a lot of responsibility for taking care of my mom. Learning about your birth order personality traits is a unique way of exploring how you relate to your own family. What you discover about yourself may surprise you.

MARRIAGES OF PARENTS & FAMILY

Tim and I both have parents who are still married to each other. They are also first marriages for both of them. There is something admirable about the commitment they share. In a later chapter, I share more about how easy divorce has become. Sticking together when things aren't perfect is actually the hard thing to do. I will speak for myself and say that growing up with parents who were still married was a rare thing. Many of my classmates came from divorced families and at times I even felt ostracized by them for the fact that my parents were still together. Most of my social circle in high school had divorced parents, living with one parent one week and the other one the next. Taking it even further than that, all of my aunts and uncles on both sides of my family have experienced divorce. You may have pain from growing up in a divorced household. You may have been divorced yourself. While that is not something I can personally relate to, I have seen a lot of divorce. I learned a lot from the deterioration of my brother's first marriage. I also learned a lot watching my brother experience the redemption that came with his second marriage.

I am proud of the longevity of my parents' marriage. If there is anything about their marriage that may serve as a caution for your own it is this: my mom and dad are not "equally yoked." There are many who may think that this whole equally yoked thing is not a big deal. This perception increases as singles get older and the pickings seem to dwindle. Let me just say, if you are a person of faith, it matters a great deal. One of the things I remember about my mom growing up was her waiting for my dad to come to desire a deeper faith. While he is and was a believer, she hoped that he would go to church with her or even join a bible study with her. My mom finally came to the decision not to wait for him and took ownership of her own spiritual growth. Once she decided to go back to church, bible study, prayer groups, etc. on her own, her faith soared. I have no doubt that my mom's faith is a witness to my dad. He has seen how tithing has blessed them. My dad has seen how her faith has helped in part to restore her mental health. Unfortunately, until my dad decides to dig deeper for himself, my mom's faith alone can't carry the both of them, though the Holy Spirit can do a mighty work. Ecclesiastes 4:9-12 is often used in wedding ceremonies and for good reason:

> *Two are better than one, because they have a good return for their labor: If either of them falls down, one can help the other up. But pity anyone who falls and has no one to help them up. Also, if two*

lie down together, they will keep warm. But how can one keep warm alone? Though one may be overpowered, two can defend themselves. A cord of three strands is not quickly broken. (New Living Translation)

When my dad's foundation shakes, my mom is there with the hope of Jesus to stand on. What happens when my mom's foundation shakes? My dad does not have that same stability to offer her so she has to find it outside of him through friends and other family. There is no promise that marriages that are "equally yoked" are going to make it through all things. Sticking together is a choice both spouses have to make—but when a husband and wife are led by the Holy Spirit together, there is strength in numbers. With that said, my parents have supported each other, shortcomings and all, for over 40 years. Would being more spiritually equal make their marriage stronger? I believe so. However, their commitment to each other in the face of their differences speaks volumes to me.

UNDERSTANDING YOUR COMMUNICATION STYLE

There are four basic communication styles:

Passive, aggressive, passive-aggressive, and assertive.

Passive communicators tend to avoid expressing their true feelings and are quick to yield to others. Aggressive communicators tend to speak loudly, even rudely, and fail to listen to the opinions of others. Passive-aggressive communicators tend to be passive on the surface, but build up resentment that leads to subtle aggressive behaviors. Assertive communicators tend to be the most effective because they are free to express their ideas and feelings while striving for balance with others. Can you already begin to identify your own communication style? In most situations I am somewhere between assertive and aggressive. I am not proud of the aggressive part and try to lean toward assertive. We call that *"being a Renaud"* in my family. Tim, on the other hand, is more passive; sliding over to assertive when he is passionate about something or knows he is right about something. He is not naturally assertive, whereas I am assertive by default. For example, he would never send food back at a restaurant and I have no problem addressing an issue with the manager.

Personality can impact communication style, however, a lot about how we communicate is at least influenced by our families. We had conversations early in our relationship about our communication styles. One of the big things we talked about was my dislike for being corrected. I am open to criticism and being corrected when I was wrong about something. What I truly dislike is being corrected when there is not really a need for it. It was important for us to talk about that issue and where it stemmed from. When I was growing up, there was no arguing with my dad. He has really strong opinions about almost everything. After all, he is more *"Renaud"* than anyone in my family. I honestly do get a lot of my assertiveness (and a pinch of my aggressiveness) from him. When I would express an opinion or thought, if he really didn't agree with me, he would tell me just how much. There would also be times when he would find it necessary to correct me, even if I was right. He would word things in his own way or *mansplain*.[2]

Initially, I accused Tim of *mansplain-ing* something to me when he was simply trying to clarify. His intent was to clarify what I was saying in order to better understand me. When he would do that, I would hear it as a correction. I would become really defensive and accuse him of correcting me. It upset him that I was upset, so we really had to talk about it. Learning how your partner communicates will go a long way to avoid unnecessary hurt and conflict. Additionally, learning how you communicate and being able to express yourself effectively will actually help you avoid conflict in all types of relationships.

Growing up the way I did, speaking up for myself was something I had to learn to do. Once I was able to find my voice, I didn't want to lose it again. Thankfully, Tim respects my thoughts and opinions. On the other hand, I am still a product of my upbringing where speaking freely wasn't always celebrated. This means I also have tendencies to shut down when I do not feel free. Specifically, I shut down when I am trying to avoid conflict and want to damper a situation. It is also a defense mechanism that isn't very productive for solving issues.

Growing up, I was the peacekeeper at home. I did whatever I could behind the scenes to prevent any conflict I saw coming. I even went as far as to cover up for my brothers. Peacekeepers who work hard to not rock the boat are actually experiencing a trauma response. When I try to keep the peace now, I am actually responding to how I felt when I was younger and the conflict that was going on around me. I thought I was making things more peaceful by trying to keep the peace. However, there's a big difference between being a peace*keeper* and a peace*maker* (Matthew 5:9). Peacekeepers try to maintain peace by avoiding conflict. There tends to be a peacekeeper in every family. Perhaps it was you! Peacemakers on the other hand are willing to walk into a conflict in order to establish peace. Learning to fight well, or rather, work through conflict in a healthy way is a very important skill in any relationship.

ENMESHMENT & BOUNDARIES IN FAMILIES

When someone is single, there is an odd sense of obligation within his or her family of origin. There is no rulebook for how a single adult is supposed to behave or function in a family. Scripture really only describes what happens in families when a person gets married:

> *"A man leaves his father and mother and is joined to his wife, and the two are united into one"* Genesis 2:24 NLT

There's this idea that singles are just supposed to default to "honor thy father and mother" and become one with the original family unit until marriage. I have talked to several singles about the role they play in their families. Each of them describes feeling obligated to be available whenever called upon by their parents, married siblings, or nieces and nephews. When not careful, relationships within a family can become enmeshed or entangled. A great example of an enmeshed family is the Tanner family on *Full House*. Don't get me wrong; I loved *Full House* growing up. While it is supposed to be a good-hearted sitcom about a close-knit family, if you look closer, there is enmeshed behavior all over the place. Uncle Jesse had to live in the attic with his wife and twin boys for goodness sake! Even the idea of leaving the home to pursue his wife and family was met with a lot of drama, tears, and honestly, manipulation.

A truly enmeshed family is an unhealthy family because enmeshment involves blurred or nonexistent boundaries, unhealthy patterns, control and manipulation, and a lack of independence and individuality.[3] In my counseling practice, I see a lot of issues that stem from family enmeshment. When healthy boundaries aren't taught or shown in a family, healthy boundaries are usually never practiced as an adult. A lack of boundaries also produces

---

[.] Zwick, J, et al (Directors). (1987–1995). *Full House* [Television series]. Burbank, CA: American Broadcasting Company (ABC).

resentment, bitterness, and anger toward the person who is violating a boundary. However, when there are no defined boundaries, you can't expect people to honor them. The other concern with enmeshment is this learned behavior can carry over into romantic relationships. In romantic relationships, enmeshment looks more like codependency, which is excessive emotional reliance on a romantic partner.

SIGNS OF ENMESHMENT INCLUDE:
1. When a family member is feeling angry, sad, or anxious, you begin to exhibit the same emotions without cause.
2. Your own happiness is contingent on the happiness of a family member.
3. How you feel about yourself (self-esteem) is contingent on how your family member is feeling about you.
4. You may be neglecting other relationships in your life including friends, coworkers, romantic relationships, etc. because of a preoccupation to always be available for a family member.
5. When conflict arises with a family member, you have a compulsion to fix the problem and experience immense anxiety when you can't.
6. Lack of communication with a family member causes you to feel irrationally lonely or you experience immense desire to reconnect with them.

If you recognize enmeshment in your family of origin, you will want to work on creating healthy boundaries now. Here are some steps to take to begin setting boundaries with enmeshed family members:
1. Seek professional help to heal any underlying issues feeding the enmeshment. Family counseling may also be explored.

2. Begin establishing boundaries with enmeshed family members that shows you still love them, but are respectful to your own personal limits.
3. Create new connections outside of your family relationships in order to establish healthy space between your personal life and your family life.

At the end of the day, you don't get to pick your family, but you do get to pick how involved in your life they are. Toula Portokalos came to realize at the end of *My Big Fat Greek Wedding*, the family she has is the family she has. They are big, loud, and in her business all the time. In the end, she embraced it. What she didn't do was learn to create healthy boundaries with them, especially as she entered into a marriage relationship. It wasn't until she was facing marriage that she started to create boundaries. In large part, that is why it was so hard for her family to adjust. As you consider dating and marriage, learning to leave and cleave into your own individuality is a skill to work on now. Creating healthy boundaries with your family today will aid in your ability to create more boundaries later.

ABUSE IN FAMILIES

While every family has issues of some kind, not every family is safe to remain a part of. There are circumstances that even firmer boundaries need to be put in place. That may mean ending some family relationships entirely. If you come from an abusive family, you are allowed to create space and separation to protect yourself. Forgiving your family for any past abuse is necessary in order to release yourself from the hurt. Forgiveness, however, is not always a step toward reconciliation and it doesn't have to be.

FAMILY MATTERS QUESTIONS

Parental Issues

Who mainly raised you as a child and adolescent?

Parents

What was it like growing up in your home?

Good   loving   Secure

Were there any major events that occurred within your family as you were growing up? (divorces, deaths, etc.)

nothing memorable

Describe your parents' relationship while you were growing up.

Seemed healthy

What is your parents' relationship like today?

Dad is gone

What aspects of your parents' marriage(s) or relationship(s) would you like to emulate?

? - ?

What aspects of your parents' marriage(s) or relationship(s) will you avoid?

Control / Debt Roles?

How do your parents violate your personal boundaries?

Can you identify any enmeshment in your relationship with your parents?

my mom can be too (personally) involved at times

What boundaries do you need to establish with your parents?

Speak up in loving ways

Family Issues

How many siblings do you have?

2 - alive
1 - in Heaven

Where do you fall in the birth/age order?

Baby

Did you get along with your family while you were growing up?

Yes

Do you get along with your family of origin today?

Yes

Which members of your family are you close to?

Bros

Are there any family members that are a problem for you?

not any more, I've changed

Growing up, were you a peacekeeper or a peacemaker?

neither baby & brat probably

How did your family communicate growing up?

alot well

How would you describe your communication style today?

Better less stuborn

How do your siblings violate your personal boundaries?

Perversion

Can you identify any enmeshment with your siblings?

not any more

Have you experienced abuse within your family?

not aware of any

If you experienced abuse in your family, what does your relationship with your abuser(s) look like today?

What boundaries do you need to establish with your siblings or other family members?

Chapter 5:
You Are Allowed to Have a Past
(Your Spouse Will Have One Too)

"Oh yes, the past can hurt. But, you can either run from it or learn from it." Rafiki, The Lion King[*]

Everyone has baggage. Some bags are bigger, some smaller. Some baggage is painful while other baggage is embarrassing. While the details differ, there is not a person alive or dead who doesn't have a past. Dealing with your past through forgiveness, humility, and honesty is the best way to leave the baggage behind. Shortly before I met Tim, I thought I had found the one I was going to marry. It sounds almost ridiculous to say now because Tim is

---

[*] Hahn., D. (Producer), & Allers, R. & Minkoff, R. (Directors). (1994). *The Lion King* [Motion Picture].

beyond anything I could have hoped for in a boyfriend, fiancé, and now as a husband and best friend. In fact, it is difficult to write this part of my story because I do not like to think of anyone having come before him. I don't even like to admit there was anyone before him. For many of you reading this, you too may have people in your past that you may not be so happy to say are there. No matter how you see them, they are a part of your story. As for me, I was in a long-distance, online dating relationship with a guy from West Virginia. Our relationship only consisted of texts, emails, and phone calls.

While we never met in person, we had a lot of meaningful conversations about our lives and our hopes for the future. We even had conversations about any willingness there was for one of us to move closer to the other in the event that the relationship progressed toward marriage. We seemed to have a lot in common on the surface and the conversations we had felt easy. He said all the right things at a time in my life that I felt desperate to hear it all. I admit that I most assuredly gave my heart away to this guy much too quickly. The idea of guarding my heart (Proverbs 4:23) was not even a thought—it definitely should have been. Had I guarded my heart, I could have avoided a lot of hurt.

One day out of the blue this *"man of my dreams"* ghosted me. For those who do not know what *ghosted* means, it is a relatively new, perhaps even millennial term. It is basically when the person you are dating discontinues all communication without warning and without explanation. One minute they are there and the next they are gone—like a ghost in the wind. In the case of my ghosting experience, he stopped returning my texts and no longer accepted my calls. He also unfriended me on Facebook, where we had just become *Facebook Official* the week before. We went from chatting about the future to literally never hearing from him again. Initially, it wrecked me as I wondered what I did wrong.

I never expected something like that to happen to me. I wondered what I could have done to prevent it because obviously in my mind it *had* to have been about *me. He had been so perfect up until then, right?* With my lack of dating experience, the things he said to me and how he said them were new, exciting, and hopeful—including the L word. That's right, he even said he loved me. I personally never said it back because I could not shake the feeling that something was not quite right. I assumed that feeling meant it was just too soon for love. However, had my discernment been working right, that should have been a red flag right there. The problem with being desperate for love and to be in a relationship is that the right things can sound more right than they really are.

LEARNING FROM THE PAST

The reason I share this part of my story is as a word of warning: please do not give your heart away too soon. Let me be an example to you. I gave my heart away too soon, had it get broken, and as a result I was scared to trust again. When Tim came along shortly thereafter, I had to admit that I was recently coming off of a difficult experience and that my heart was tender. Tim also had to reconcile his own insecurities of feeling a little like a rebound (which he was not). I did learn a great deal from that whole experience. There's a part of me that believes I needed to go through that in order to be ready for when the real thing (my husband Tim) came along. My hope is that you don't have to go through all of that in order to learn the same lesson. You must practice good discernment about the person you are dating.

When you give your heart away too soon, your head stops thinking and your tender (stupid) little heart takes over. I will just say it—your heart cannot be trusted. Love is a choice—not a feeling. Hear me again: love is a choice—not a feeling. When you first meet someone and hit it off, it is not love that you are feeling. The excitement and passion you feel is a combination of brain chemicals: dopamine, serotonin, oxytocin, and endorphins. These chemicals are designed to bond you to another person. They can also cloud good, rational judgment. Once the "love" drugs wear off, love absolutely becomes a choice. You will have to choose each and every day to love your spouse. As long as you are intentional about putting your relationship first, the choice to love won't feel like much of a choice at all.

LET'S TALK PURITY (I SAW THAT EYE ROLL!)

It is easy to want to skip over this section. Even roll your eyes at the thought of another discussion on purity. One of the worst things that came out of purity culture was the idea that if you did everything *just right* (court and not date around, abstain from pre-marital sex, and the lot) that God will bless you with a loving spouse, a strong marriage, and a healthy family. As if purity was the secret to happiness and wholeness. Unfortunately, there is a line at divorce court full of people who bought into that and found themselves deeply disappointed. They discovered that life did not turn out how they were promised. There was still pain. There was still sadness. There was still betrayal. There was still sickness. There was still death.

The problem with the promise given by purity culture is that we should actually follow God's standard for purity because we love Him, worship Him, and wish to obey Him. We shouldn't follow God's standard because we expect a payout at the end of the day. At least that is how it is supposed to work. We are only promised two things on this side of heaven: 1) in this world you will have trouble (John 16:33) and 2) Jesus will make all things new (Revelation 21:5). These promises mean that life isn't always going to be rainbows and puppies, but we can take heart in knowing that all things will one day be made new.

IF YOU STRUGGLE WITH PORN, DEAL WITH IT NOW...

As a former porn addict, I would be doing you a disservice if I did not at least address pornography addiction in this book. Roughly 50% of men and 30% of women struggle with some form of pornography addiction. Among Christian communities, porn serves as a purity security blanket of sorts. Many Christians turn to pornography and masturbation in order to avoid sexual intercourse. There is a belief among single, Christian porn users that if they could just get married they would not need to use pornography anymore. There could not be anything further from the truth. Whatever you struggle with before you get married, if you do not deal with it, it will come with you into your marriage. When it comes to pornography addiction or even compulsive masturbation issues, those issues become exponentially compounded once an addict becomes married. Marriage is not a license to do whatever you want sexually, including masturbation and pornography. In marriage, sex is only a part of physical intimacy with a spouse and of course is also a means of procreation.

There is no physical requirement for sexual release whether you are single or married. Meaning, no one has died because they were deprived of an orgasm. This is true for women and for men. There is a reckless myth that says if men do not masturbate that they will explode, but the truth is, the human body has a natural way to release the build up of semen without masturbation or sexual intercourse. The desire to have an orgasm without a sexual partner is a physiological response to prolonged exposure to certain brain chemicals. When you have an orgasm, four brain chemicals are released in the pleasure center of the brain (the same ones that release when you fall in love): dopamine, serotonin, oxytocin, and endorphins. These are designed to bond you to another person during sex. When these chemicals are released without a sexual partner, the bonding occurs to the pornography or the fantasy that is used during masturbation. That is why pornography, fantasy, and especially masturbation become so addictive. Masturbation is something that is hotly debated in both Christian and addiction recovery circles. Some say it is fine while other say it isn't. In my way of thinking, anything that causes you to bond sexually with anything other than a marriage partner is obviously not productive to your recovery (to porn, fantasy, etc.).

Masturbation is not something I recommend for singles or even in marriage (outside of marital intimacy) because sex is not designed by God to be a solo act. It was not right for Adam to be alone… I can only imagine why God said that, but He created Eve for Adam on purpose. For those may have a compulsive need or an addiction to masturbation, go just 90 days without it. Alcoholics Anonymous or other twelve step groups recommend, 90 meetings in 90 days because in recovery, 90 days is the sweet detox window to create new, positive habits. 90 days without an orgasm will allow your mind and body to reset from the release of the pleasure center brain chemicals that you have become addicted to. When you achieve the 90 days, you may not even have the desire to begin again. That's the hope.

When you give porn up or masturbation, you may need to grieve. You have to say goodbye to the thing that brought you comfort (or at least perceived comfort) for a long time. You are saying goodbye to isolation, and hello to healthy connection.

(RE)COMMITTING TO ABSTINENCE

For a lot of people who have already had sex in the past and are no longer virgins, it becomes easier to continue that pattern of behavior in a new relationship. There is an unfortunate belief that since one's virginity has gone out the window already (whether many years ago as a teen or even in your most recent relationship), there is no reason to pretend otherwise. There is good news though. There is no reason why this pattern has to continue. No matter what may be in your past, there is grace enough to cover it. It is never too late to honor your future spouse by recommitting to abstinence from sex going forward. You also honor your future spouse by being honest about your past.

While you can't change what has happened physically, you can become a virgin again in your soul and in your mind. The idea of re-virginizing sounds hokey when you call it that, however, all it really means is you are making the decision to wait until you are married to have sex again. It is that simple. Deciding to commit or recommit to abstinence doesn't happen once you are in a relationship. It happens now. Regardless of religious beliefs, abstinence is considered beneficial for a number of other reasons: safeguarding from sexually transmitted diseases, prevention of unplanned pregnancy, and of course, it boosts non-sexual intimacy with a partner.

Outside of purity culture, we also live in a secular culture that says everything that is consensual between the persons involved should be accepted and allowed. When we assert our Christian beliefs, especially when it relates to sex, it is received with the very same judgment our culture tells us that we are not allowed to have for others who differ. Desiring to be abstinent again or admitting one is still a virgin is often met with mockery. Even in television and movies, it is the virgin that is represented as the nerd who is out of town with reality. 1 Corinthians 10:3 says, *"Everything is permissible, but not everything is beneficial."* God gave free will to all of us. He desired for us to choose to obey, not to thrust His will upon us. As a result, you are free to do whatever you want (within the limit of city, state, and federal laws). The kicker is that while you are free to do whatever you want, not everything you decide to do is beneficial or God's best for your life. If you desire to live your life like Christ, then the standard for purity doesn't change just because something gets hard... er... difficult. Let me just say, it is much harder to hold onto principles of virtue and valor than to give into the pressures of society. There is no doubt though that the wait is worth it.

Most of what I have discussed in this chapter has to do with past relationships and sexuality. I do know that there are definitely other issues to consider. Some people have struggled with serial dating and relationships. Some have struggled with drugs or alcohol. Some have struggled with pornography and sexual sin. Some have struggled with self-esteem and worth. Others have even struggled with all of it. The most important thing to remember is that you are allowed to have a past, but it is not okay to stay there. Just as God loves you and loves you unconditionally, He loves you too much to have you stay there. All things are forgiven and covered by the grace of God.

Healing from your past through counseling, forgiveness, and authenticity is the only way to escape it. Since it is okay for you to have a past, it is also okay for whoever you marry to have a past as long as they have received healing too. In a later chapter, you will be asked to think about the kind of person you wish to date. You probably wouldn't like someone eliminating you as a potential spouse because of an issue in your past. Remember to have grace on this journey for yourself and the person you will one day marry: *"Above all, love each other [and yourself] deeply, because love covers over a multitude of sins."* 1 Peter 4:8.

EXPLORING YOUR PAST QUESTIONS

What baggage from your past do you still carry around with you?

warped identity

What do you need to let go of in order to move forward?

rejection + abandonment

Where have you seen the permissible things not be so beneficial in your life?

Do you want to wait until marriage to have sex? If so, why is that important to you?

Yes to bond correctly

If you haven't been abstinent in the past, how will you commit to it in the future?

In pray + accountability

Has porn (or erotica) ever been an issue for you? If so, what steps do you take to stay free from it?

Renounce masturbation + more aware of how it harms me

How have you been negatively impacted by purity culture?

Of corse

How many dating relationships have you had? If you don't date, what has kept you from pursuing relationships?

?

Have you ever been married? If so, why did that marriage end?

Yes twice Divorced twice

What does dating look like in your life right now?

non existant

Can you think of a time when you gave your heart away to someone too quickly?

every man I've ever been with.

Why did your last relationship end?

Divorce — my self righteous attitude — Alcohol Drugs Bad Women

What did you learn from your last relationship?

To seek God alone for my identity + worth

Is there anything from your past you are already worried to share with a potential spouse?

no

What other issues reside in your past that you are afraid, ashamed, or embarrassed to admit are there?

None – I'm an open book

What steps do you need take now to begin healing the issues of your past?

Continued prayer + surrender + honesty w/ God

Section Two:
DATING

Chapter 6:
Kiss Dating Hello

"Are you free for dinner tonight?" "Yes." "Alright, then it's a date."
Jim & Pam, The Office

    In section one, I discussed the first reason I had for writing this book—getting singles comfortable with being single. Now, the second reason for writing this book is to help a dating couple navigate the many aspects of a relationship—from first dates to wedding dates. It wasn't all that long ago that I was waiting for someone to come along and ask me out. Before I met Tim, I remember saying to my friend Jenny, *"Is it too much to ask to meet a local guy who will take me out for a free dinner?"* Even better would

---

* Kwapis, K. (Director). (2007). The Job. [Television series episode] In Bright, Reveille Productions and Deedle-Dee Productions (Producers), *The Office*. New York City, NY: NBC Universal Television.

have been to be handed a *bouquet of newly sharpened pencils* that day too (a nod to my favorite movie). I know it sounds terrible to say I wanted to be taken out for a free dinner. There's honestly no rule that says the guy has to even pay for dinner. For me though, I longed for the first date experience that most young women long for. At nearly 33 years old, I had never experienced it before, not even at a school dance. I was growing impatient! However, there is so much more to dating than getting a free meal.

DATING IS NOT THE BAD GUY

Between a first date and a wedding date, there is a lot to consider along the way. First, let's define some things. The first thing I want to do is help redeem the concept of dating. For whatever reason, in the late 1990s, Christian leaders convinced a lot of young people to do away with the term *dating* in favor of the more traditional terms, *courting* or *courtship*. Apparently, dating has grown to have too many negative connotations, especially as it pertains to purity. In the last two decades, however, the term *courtship* has also been given a bad reputation. You might think of courtship as an old fashioned, outdated relationship model and you might be right.

When one hears the word *courtship*, they may think of the reality TV family, the Duggars. In their family, courting is a relationship stage a couple enters into that is focused on getting to know one another with marriage in mind. Most adult couples don't really involve their parents until engagement comes up. This type of courting however requires the man go to a woman's father to ask permission to court her. This type of courting also requires strict physical boundaries where the only acceptable physical contact is side hugs, and maybe hand holding after engagement. Kissing is almost exclusively reserved for the wedding day. In this type of courting, a couple is also *never* allowed to be alone in person, even after they have become engaged. All of their dates and time spent together must have a chaperone present though they are allowed to communicate by phone, video chat, etc. in private.

When you hear the word courting, you may also think of a book from the late 1990s called, *I Kissed Dating Goodbye* by author and ex-pastor Joshua Harris. *I Kissed Dating Goodbye* became the would-be textbook for purity culture in the late 1990s into the early 2000s. In his book, Harris shares his story of giving up dating in exchange for a life of sincere love, true purity, and purposeful singleness. He was just 21 years old at the time of first publication. I thought I was young publishing my first book at 26! His follow up title, *Boy Meets Girl: Say Hello to Courtship* was a retelling of his own courtship story. In it, he encouraged young Christians to embrace courtship like he did if they were going to pursue a relationship at all. At the same time I am knee deep writing this book, a firestorm has recently taken place with Harris at the center of it. After 20 years of marriage, Harris and his wife announced they are getting divorced. In addition to that, Harris announced he was turning away from the Christian faith he had followed the entirety of his life. This came roughly a year after Harris denounced his bestselling book, *I Kissed Dating Goodbye*. Harris' decision to denounce his first book was one I was actually happy and surprised to see.

An entire generation of young Christians clung to Harris' advice but was ultimately left hurt. They realized that purity culture set them up for failure, not unlike what I discussed in Chapter 1. Doing all of the *right* things was not a promise for a lifetime of happiness. However, Harris did not create purity culture. He was taught it, grew up in it, and believed it for himself that it was right… until he stopped. Harris grew up with extremely conservative parents and he ran with the purity culture narrative. By denouncing the book, he apologized to all those the book ultimately hurt and even halted any further printings of it. Unfortunately, his path to repairing purity culture did not stop at denouncing his book—but was the beginning of him kissing Christianity goodbye altogether.[7]

As someone who doesn't know the man at all, all I can do is speculate as to the root of why he came to this decision. I don't think Harris ever experienced true grace or vulnerability in his relationship with God and others. I believe that once he began to see the damage his legalistic past had caused, he could not find a balance. It became all or nothing. To him, there could not be Christianity with grace, or purity with grace. I hold no ill will toward Harris personally. In fact, it is my prayer that God meets Harris right where he is. I pray God reveals to him the heart of a Father that He has for all prodigal sons and daughters: filled with conviction, mercy, grace, forgiveness, and love.

COURTING VS DATING

According to the Institute for Basic Life Principles (the organization deeply followed by the Duggar family), *"In a dating relationship, self-gratification is normally the basis of the relationship. Instead of focusing on God's pleasure, the couple is often looking for personal pleasure. This oblivious self-centeredness can lead only to dissatisfaction, promoting an attitude of lust (taking what I want) rather than the Scriptural attitude of love (giving unselfishly to others)."*[8] Presumptions aside, courtship is actually defined as *"a period during which a couple develops a romantic relationship, especially with a view to marriage."*[9] Or as it were… *Dating Done Right*. Whether you want to call it dating or courting, the big difference is the set of rules that tends to follow conservative courtship ideals. Courtship is putting up walls so you never get to know the other person for who they really are until after marriage. That is problematic! Getting to know someone you may potentially marry requires intimate conversations you cannot have with a chaperone hanging around. Can you imagine talking about the good, the bad, and the ugly of your past and your hopes and dreams for the future, all within earshot of your little brother or sister? You simply cannot get to know someone the way you need to know them through chaperoned or group dates. If all you ever see is how someone acts in front of someone else, you are only seeing someone at their very best. You certainly won't get anywhere by avoiding dating all together.

I do believe one of the reasons dating has been given a bad reputation is all of the terrible dating advice people have been given. Bad dating advice leads to bad dating outcomes. It is just that simple. I asked my survey takers what were the best and worst dating advice they'd been given and here at the top ten results:

TEN WORST DATING TIPS

Just put yourself out there more.
Stop being so picky.
Date as many people as you can to find the right one.
Lower your expectations.
It's okay to lie about yourself a little.
Wait three days to call her back.
Let them make the first move.
If you stop wanting it, God will bring them to you.
Don't put all your eggs in one basket.
It will happen when you least expect it.

> # TEN BEST DATING TIPS
> Don't play games.
> Know you who you are and what you want.
> Don't judge the future by the past.
> Above all, guard your heart.
> Keep an open mind, but don't settle.
> When you know, you know.
> Communicate. Communicate. Communicate.
> Don't change yourself for someone else.
> Pray for your future spouse.
> Learn from the experience.
> It's better to wait long than to marry wrong.

DATING WITHOUT REGRETS

I don't want it to seem like all I do is pick on the Duggars. I actually really enjoy *Counting On* and watched several seasons for inspiration while writing this book. They are a sweet family who I believe have good intentions—though I believe the patriarch has too much control over his adult kids. I do want to mention one thing that the Duggar (adult) kids often say that I think is actually worth repeating. They say they adhere to their strict courtship rules because they have a desire to live their lives in such a way as to not have regrets. While they go to extremes to achieve this goal, don't miss the essence of that. You *can* date without regrets and you *should* go into dating with that goal. I believe in being wise in all ways when it comes to dating, but dating is not wrong. In fact, dating should be encouraged. Dating is most definitely not all about

---

· Enlow, S. (Director). (2015–Present). *Counting On* [Television series]. Tontitown, AR: TLC.

self-gratification, personal pleasure, or an attitude of lust. Dating is an important part of the process of building a friendship first and eventually, a lasting relationship with another person.

I am not an advocate for serial dating. I am not an advocate for dating for the sake of dating. I am not an advocate for first dates that end in first kisses (and then some). I am not advocate for dating more than one person at a time. I am not an advocate for settling for less than you deserve. I am not an advocate for compromising purity standards. I am, however, an advocate for dating biblically and in a God-honoring way. A lot can be learned through the process of dating. What is most important is to remember that dating is not marriage. In the same way, dating should not have the same perks that come with marriage. Dating is an excellent opportunity to practice boundaries. Practicing physical, emotional, and spiritual boundaries in dating will aid in safeguarding the relationship from regrets. These boundaries begin before a first date is even planned because they start in your own heart.

Dating Done Right is about encouraging dating couples to get vulnerable with each other. The heart of it is not to casually date or be pressured to marry fast—but to pursue a relationship on purpose with marriage in mind. In the chapters to come, I hope to help dating couples to do just that.

KISS DATING HELLO QUESTIONS

What are some of your preconceived ideas about courting?

What are some of your preconceived ideas about dating?

Where did you learn your philosophy of dating?

Has your philosophy of dating changed? If so, how?

What would you say are the benefits of dating vs. courting?

What is the worst dating advice you've ever been given? Why?

What is the best dating advice you've ever been given? Why?

What physical boundaries do you need to commit to before you begin dating?

What emotional boundaries do you need to commit to before you begin dating?

What spiritual boundaries do you need to commit to before you begin dating?

Chapter 7:
Finding Someone Worth Falling For

"It's not who you want to spend Friday night with. It's who you want to spend all day Saturday with." Tommy, Friends with Benefits[*]

    Do you remember the childhood game M.A.S.H.? From what kind of home you would live in to how many kids you would have, this classic game would predict your future. The options were all based on things you picked for yourself: names of your crushes, the kind of cars you like, what pets you prefer, etc. The only real risk in the game was ending up in a shack. M.A.S.H. was a fun game in elementary school, but it was obviously incredibly unrealistic. We do not get to pick what we want that easily, as if picking our ideal life off a menu. The same is true for the person

---

[*] Glotzer, L., Gluck, W., Shafer, M., Zucker, J, & Zucker, J. (Producers), & Gluck, W. (Director). (2011). *Friends with Benefits* [Motion Picture].

you will date and marry. The man of your dreams probably won't ride into your life on a white horse. The woman you desire probably won't be a damsel in distress. If one of those two is what you are waiting for, you might end up with more of a *Shrek* situation. You cannot predict your future or even plan too heavily. Especially who your spouse will be or how many kids you may one day have. However, it is absolutely within your power to think about and pray about your future spouse and what kind of person they will be. Consider the song, *"Prayed for You"* performed by Matt Stell:[10]

Every single day, before I knew your name
I couldn't see your face, but I prayed for you
Every heartbreak trail when all hope fell
On the highway to hell, I prayed for you
I kept my faith like that old King James said I'm supposed to
It's hard to imagine, bigger than I could fathom
I didn't know you from Adam but I prayed for you

Praying for your future spouse is one of the best ways to prepare for them. While you do not know their name, their hair or eye color, their hopes or dreams, you can pray for them. Praying for them does a couple of things: 1) it keeps your mind focused on what you want in a spouse and 2) by keeping your mind focused on what you want, the less likely you are to settle for what you don't want. Most people know the well-loved and well-worn verse that says, *"God will give you the desires of your heart."* From Psalm 37:4, this verse is often used to encourage singles waiting for marriage. Perhaps you have had people recite it to you on your journey of singleness. The problem with it is the idea that God is up in Heaven waiting to give us whatever we think we want. The verse is actually more intentional than that. The full verse reads, *"Delight yourself in the Lord, and he will give you the desires of your heart"* Psalm 37:4 ESV.

When you delight yourself in the Lord, you are actually taking the focus off of what you want in order to long for what He wants for you. When that happens, His desires for us become our own. Keep in mind that when you pray for your future spouse, God is already working out the details. He is mindful of what you desire, but He knows much better than you do what it is you actually need in a partner. The right person will complement your weaknesses and you will complement theirs. What you truly need in a spouse should have nothing to do with how they look or how much money they make—they should have everything to do with their character, their integrity, and above all, their devotion to God.

HAPPILY EVER AFTER TAKES WORK

The whole "and they lived happily ever after" thing is not always so blissfully achieved. A whole generation of young girls were served incredibly high expectations about men from Disney princesses, and the princes who rescued them. Let's talk about the actress Meghan Markle, now known as the Duchess of Sussex. Her story may seem like a fairytale. After all, she was just an American girl set up on a blind date by a friend. Little did she know that her blind date would turn out to be with Prince Harry of the British Royal family. A year later, she was engaged to be married. It sounds like something out of a Disney movie, right? Not quite. Instead of planning a wedding with her mother and friends, she was to undergo a crash course in "princess training" in order to be accepted at the royal court.[11]

The truth of the matter is, falling in love with a prince and marrying a prince also meant great sacrifices on her part. She had to take on the responsibilities of being a part of a royal family. She had to retire from her passion of acting at the age of only 36. She had to move across the world leaving her old life in the United States behind, including friends and family. I can only imagine that even now she is struggling with some identity loss as she navigates what her new normal is. That is if there is anything normal about being a royal. Recently, she was interviewed and tearfully expressed while talking about being a newlywed and now a new mother, "Not many people have asked if I'm okay."[12] Falling in love is wonderful. Committing to someone in marriage is a beautiful thing. Though it often comes with some sacrifices. You may not have to move across the world for love like Meghan Markle. However, marriage is a major life adjustment and you will have to make room for your spouse in not just your heart but also your every day life.

Tim loves pizza, spaghetti, lasagna... basically every marinara-laced Italian dish there is. I, on the other hand, cannot stand red sauce. From the time I was very young, I cringed at the taste of marinara sauce, even on pizza. Growing up, my mom would go as far as to set aside and serve me plain spaghetti noodles with butter and garlic before smothering the rest with meat sauce. Upon learning this about me, Tim worried he may never get to enjoy a red sauce soaked meal ever again. Thankfully for him there is some compromise. One example is, when I work late nights at the counseling office or am out of town without him, he will make himself spaghetti and red sauce and enjoy it to his heart's content. He regularly denies himself meals he loves because he knows I will not enjoy it with him. While that may not seem like much of a sacrifice, it is for Tim. He is making accommodations for me and my likes and dislikes. Another small sacrifice that I make for Tim is, while I love suspenseful dramas and even horror movies with zombies and psychopaths, he really does not do well with them. He has far too much empathy to handle watching people suffer for fun. As for me, I am fine going without so that we can watch movies and shows together. We are both movie buffs, so we can usually find something to watch that we can both enjoy.

Let's take things a bit further. Accommodations for a spouse aren't just about food aversions and movie preferences. Imagine if you fell in love with someone who is physically handicapped or hard of hearing. Imagine if you fell in love with someone who comes from a cultural or racial background significantly different from your own. Not all accommodations are easy, but they are necessary in order for the relationship to work. Dating is not all dinners out and kisses at the door. If you are dating right, it means a lot of real life experiences getting you prepared for real life marriage. While we never lived together, during our engagement we began to live as though we were already married. We joined our bank accounts together, began budgeting together, and stopped making plans without considering the other person.

Dates are not all fun and games either. Dates will sometimes mean grocery shopping and running errands together. A funny story from my parents' dating relationship was on one of their first dates, they went to the store. My mom needed tampons and that apparently seemed as good a time as any to get them. My dad bought them for her! Dates may also mean bringing your girlfriend soup because she is sick and can't go out or bringing your boyfriend Gatorade because he got dehydrated. Both were occurrences while Tim and I were dating. Relationships require times of putting the other person's needs before your own—a lot of times. If you ask some people, they would say that in relationships, the other person's needs should always come first. I tend to agree. When each spouse puts the other's needs first, they both have their needs met. Neither one is left to fend for themselves.

AGES AND LIFE STAGES

Tim and I are over four years apart in age. Traditionally, if one is older, it is usually the guy or at least that is how it seems. In our case, I am the older one. At first (and unfortunately for a little while after that), I struggled with the age gap. I personally did not know very many couples where the woman was older. I felt like an old lady, particularly because when I met Tim, I was in my 30's and he was still in his 20's. That distinction wigged me out. While I was in my 30's and he was in his 20's, there was less than five years between us. The truth of the matter an age four or five year age gap is next to nothing. Age is not a huge factor to consider when dating a potential spouse. However, there is something to be said for choosing a partner that is close enough in age to you that you have shared life experiences. For example, Tim joked that when he was considering the idea of dating, he would say that if someone could not pinpoint where she was on September 11th, then she was too young for him. (Maybe I shouldn't mention that on September 11th, I was a junior in high school and Tim was in middle school). If the person you are dating has more shared life experiences with your dad or a grandma than with you, you might want to consider if the gap is too wide for you to have enough in common. Then again, Tim drinks bourbon neat, enjoys golf, and listens to audio books. He has the soul of a 60 year old while I watch the Kansas City Royals on TV and eat dry Fruit Loops out of a cup like a toddler. Maturity levels are not always age specific.

Age can sometimes determine a person's life stage or create assumptions about someone's maturity or immaturity. Couples who are younger (under the age of 25) may need to take a little more time developing their relationship than older couples. That is not ageism; it is just fact and science. The prefrontal cortex of the human brain is responsible for personality, impulse control, rational thought, and complex behaviors. This part of the brain is not fully developed until the age of 25 or so. Picture an undercooked cupcake. It may look fully baked on the outside, but the inside is still gooey. Younger couples will need to be more diligent in practicing good discernment when dating and perhaps even seek out a mentor couple for additional support. However, discernment and support are required no matter the age. On the flip side, I used to wrongfully judge guys who were older and unmarried. I would wonder what was wrong with them. Surely, if they did not get married at a younger age, then there was something about them that was not *marriable*. Then I became older myself and realized that is not really fair.

What I have come to learn is the good guy doesn't always marry young because girls aren't necessarily looking for the good guy. They are looking for the *perfect* guy: career, car, tall, handsome. *Perfect* is summed up by what he has and looks like. The problem with that is that perfection is elusive. What is perfect at one time in your life is not so perfect later. It goes the same for men, and the women they seek out when they are younger. I will refrain from using stereotypes here, as I am sure you get the point. I would also judge men who were divorced with kids. I would say that I wanted a husband who hadn't been married before in order to avoid the baggage of exes, etc. When my brother got divorced, however, my feelings on the matter changed. He was a catch of a man whose marriage ended at really no fault of his own. He was also a really great father. I realized that if I met a man like him, I would be lucky. Automatically eliminating someone based on assumptions about their past could keep you from someone truly great.

MUST HAVES AND CAN'T STANDS

Now that we have discussed a bit about what is realistic, we can start to think about what you want in a future spouse. While some attributes are flexible (and should be), if there are attributes you know you can't stand, do not assume you can change them. If you go into a marriage-minded relationship intending to change the things you do not like about the person you are dating, you will be sorely disappointed when you come to discover you can't. When you discover you can't change them, resentment will begin to set in. With that in mind, as you consider the type of person you wish to marry, it is good to form a list of must *haves* and a list of *can't stands*. These might not be placed on literal lists, though it is good to keep them in mind.

Must haves should have nothing to do physical attributes such as height, eye color, etc. *Must haves* should have everything to do with the character of the person, including personal habits you find important. *Must haves* might also include mutual interests you hope to share with your future spouse. *Can't stands* on the other hand should also not include physical attributes such as height, eye color, etc. *Can't stands* might include bad habits such as smoking, drug use, pornography, poor hygiene, etc. *Can't stands* might also include interests that offend you or you have no interest in. However, your spouse may have interests that you aren't interested in. That does not mean they are reasons not to be together. Small differences are good while big differences may need attention.

In Chapter 3, one of the questionnaires asked if you want to have kids. How did you answer that question? Perhaps your first inclination was to say yes because kids are something we are all *supposed* to want. Perhaps your inclination was to say no because you don't like children or you are fearful you won't make a very good parent. Whatever your reason, as you consider what you want in a relationship, or rather, what you want in a person you may marry, the conversation of kids will inevitably come up. Feelings about wanting kids can change. However, if someone says they do not want kids, do not expect them to change their mind. If kids are important to you, then you need to put that on your *Must Haves* list.

FINDING SOMEONE QUESTIONS

How would you rate your maturity level? Why?

Does your maturity level match your age? If not, in what way?

How have others judged you based on your age? How?

What judgments have you made about someone's age? Why?

What judgments have you made about someone's marital history? Why?

What judgments have you made about someone's cultural or racial background? Why?

What judgments have you made about someone's physical limitations? Why?

Have your judgments or prejudices changed from what they used to be in the past? How?

What accommodations are you expecting a spouse to make for you? Why?

What accommodations do you think you would struggle making for a spouse? Why?

Create your Must Haves and Can't Stands lists

SO WHERE DO I MEET SOMEONE?

While I didn't devote an entire chapter to it, it seemed appropriate to address how to meet someone when the time comes that you are ready. People will meet in different places at different times. However, here are some possibilities based on other singles in the survey and some of my own suggestions.

Top 5 Places to Meet People (from Survey Results)
5) Local Hangout
4) Smartphone App
3) Church
2) Online
1) Through friends

Unconventional Places to Meet Other Christians
- Hobby Lobby or Chick-fil-a
- Mission Trips
- Conference or Concerts
- Serving in Ministry
- Dating Done Right Community

  Learn more at datingdonerightbook.com

Chapter 8:
The First Date

"What's your idea of a perfect date? April 25 because it's not too hot and not too cold. All you need a light jacket."
Cheryl Frasier, Miss Congeniality

There is one thing all first dates have in common: they are just plain awkward. There is no easy way around that. Even if you know the person, it is awkward. It is all a part of the process—a right of passage even. There is so much expectation wrapped up in a first date. There is so much anticipation. There is also risk, and hope of what could be. Exposing yourself to potential hurt and rejection is no small thing. All of that together is a recipe for

---

* Bullock, S. (Producer), & Petrie, D. (Director). (2000). *Miss Congeniality* [Motion Picture].

awkward. Tim and I actually made our first date a bit harder on ourselves. Online dating is fine and good, but it also makes the first date a bit more challenging. Having met online a couple of days before our first official date, Tim and I essentially ran out of things to talk about on the actual date because we had talked so much on the phone before we met. Instead of the normal small talk that naturally comes with a first date, Tim stared at me from across the table while the counselor in me berated him with whatever questions I could think of that had not already been asked on the phone. I was so awkward as I sat there unable to look back at him as he just kept staring back. I had never in my life had someone look at me the way he did. I had no idea what to do with it.

We knew we liked each other from all of the prior conversations but the pressure to perform on a first date difficult. Though our first date was awkward at times, it ultimately ended with a hug and a plan for a second date. The first date became a second, the second became a third, and the third became a forth. Each time spent together became more and more comfortable. First impressions are important, but an awkward (or even bad) first date is not indicative of a poor connection with someone. This chapter is all about helping you prepare to have the best first date possible. I am sorry though, it will be awkward no matter how well you prepare.

SAFETY FIRST DATING TIPS

First things first, no matter how you meet someone, whether it is online, through a friend, at church, or the grocery store, being safe and feeling safe on a first date is paramount. While I am not proud of it (okay, maybe I am a little), I lied to Tim on our first date. I do not recommend lying at the beginning of a relationship (or at any point in a relationship). I want you to avoid having to do what I did. Tim and I met at a restaurant on my side of town, but it was an early dinner and neither of us was really ready to end the date once the meal was over. It was also summer time, so the days were long with nightfall a long way off. The restaurant was kind of loud so sticking around there to talk also was not a great idea. We thought maybe a change of scenery might help us spark new conversation. Tim, new to the area and certainly new to my neck of the woods, asked me if there was a park nearby where we could walk around and talk for a while. The only park I knew of that was nearby was the largest, wooded park in the county—that also surrounds a 120-acre lake.

Listen, this was a first date. I had only had phone conversations with him up to this point. I was not about to take this guy to a wooded area. How was I to know whether or not he was a creepy, stalkery murderer? I didn't know so I lied and said that I did not know of any nearby parks. Blame it on his small town upbringing, but he did not seem to think it was odd to ask me go to a park with him. Granted, he did expect the only park nearby to be as big as a national park. I promise you he did not ask in a creepy way, but I certainly was not comfortable with that idea just yet. We laugh about it now because the park was literally across the main road from the restaurant. We could have walked there had we had the gumption. I tell you this story as a means of having an important discussion around safety and dating.

HERE ARE A FEW FIRST DATE SAFETY TIPS TO CONSIDER:

<u>Drive Yourself</u>

Getting picked up at your door is romantic and cute and all, but if the date turns south or you find yourself no longer feeling safe, you are stuck without a ride and your date now knows where you live. Driving yourself keeps some control in your hands. Also, remember where you park.

Choose a Public Date Location

Avoid meeting at a date location that is too isolated, such as a park or parking lot. This bit of advice is most aptly intended for online or app daters where you are essentially meeting a stranger. However, it is good advice for any type of first date. Choose a location that is well lit and well populated to keep yourself safe.

Make Sure Your Friends or Family Know Where You're Going

It is just wise to have someone know your plans. My best friend Jenny and my mom both knew where I was meeting Tim on our first date. I actually chatted with Jenny on the drive to meet Tim as she helped to keep my nerves in check. I also texted Jenny during dinner to give her updates (including a stealth picture of Tim just because she asked). At the end of the date, I called Jenny as I drove home and debriefed with her. All of these things were probably things I would have done anyway. However, if you look at them through the eyes of safety, they make sense too.

You Might Even Perform a Background Check

Performing a background check on someone you might date may seem extreme. However, we live in an age where we meet people on dating websites, over dating apps, and even on social media. Unless you meet someone through a friend or a family member, most anyone you meet will be a bit of a mystery. Perhaps even a big mystery. Before I met Tim on our first date, I knew enough about him that I was able to perform a background check online. I am not sure what I was expecting to find, but he literally had the most boring history ever. Not even a speeding ticket. That wasn't absolutely proof of a clean past but it gave me some peace of mind going into our first date. Thankfully, when I told Tim that I did this, he fully understood and jokingly just asked if I found anything interesting.

It also isn't all that unusual to stalk someone on social media before a date. As for Tim, he works in IT. As a security nerd, he is prone to doing a sweep of his own social media accounts every few months so there wasn't anything to be learned from there. A background check was really my only option as far as investigating him beforehand.

Above All, Trust Your Gut

You know instinctually when something feels off or not right. There is a reason I am encouraging you to drive yourself and have people in your life who know where you are. If something feels off, trust your gut.

SUGGESTIONS FOR GREAT FIRST DATE

The standard first date plan that is always suggested is dinner and a movie, but I cannot think of a worse idea than going to a movie on a first date. Alright, maybe there are worse ideas, but hear me out. Why would you want to do an activity that completely eliminates the ability to talk and get to know one another? I surveyed some married couples and they all agreed that the following made for the best first date activities:

- Meeting for coffee
- Enjoying a meal together—lunch or dinner
- Checking out an art festival
- Visiting a museum
- Attending a professional sports game
- Go bowling or mini golfing

QUESTIONS TO ASK ON A FIRST DATE

One piece of advice I learned too late was, if you speak to your date on the phone or by text before meeting in person, do not talk with them for hours and hours beforehand. Why do I say that? Because you will end up like Tim and I are on our first date. While we had some things to talk about, it was much harder coming up with new discussion points over dinner because we had gotten all of the first date basics out of the way before we ever met in person. The nervousness of a first date makes your head cloudy and forgetful. Do not make it harder for yourself by eliminating the basics before you ever meet. If you do decide to talk with each other before a first date, then choose an activity for your first date as opposed to just dinner. Having an activity such as bowling or mini golf, will give you something to focus on instead of sitting awkwardly over dinner. If a meal if part of your plan, then do the activity first to help break the ice and then eat.

In many ways, the first date is like an interview. You might know the equivalent of a one-sheet resumé about someone before an interview. However, it is at the interview that you discover whether someone is a good fit. With that said, here is a list of go-to first date questions to help spark some easy conversations. Try to avoid closed-ended questions that can be answered with just a yes or no response. The idea here is to create meaningful conversations, not play 20 questions.

There are a lot of questions here. You probably won't get through all of them on a first date. That is what a second, third, or even tenth dates are for.

Background Questions

- Where did you grow up?
- What is your family like?
- Are your parents still together?
- Do you have any siblings?
- What holidays did your family celebrate?
- Have you ever broken a bone or needed to have surgery?
- What was your favorite toy or game as a child?
- Did you play any instruments as a child?
- What did you enjoy most about school growing up?
- Did you go to church as a child?
- What was your high school mascot?
- What was your first job?
- Where did you go to college?
- What did you major in or study while in college?
- Have you been married before?
- Do you have any kids from a previous relationship?

Favorite Things Questions

- What is your favorite song?
- Who is your favorite musician?
- What is your favorite book?
- Who is favorite author?
- Who is your favorite actor?
- What is your favorite movie?
- What is your favorite store?
- What is your favorite drink?
- What is your favorite snack?
- What is your favorite meal of the day?
- What was your favorite meal of all time?
- What is your favorite dessert?
- What is your favorite color?
- What is your favorite smell?
- What is your favorite flower?
- What is your favorite season?
- What is your favorite holiday?
- What is your favorite scripture?

Questions for Now and for Later

- Do you go to church regularly?
- Do you pray regularly?
- Do you study the bible regularly?
- Do you believe in or have any regrets? Why?
- What motivates you to get up each morning?
- What inspires you?
- What are you most grateful for in your life?
- What do you worry too much about?
- What are your biggest fears?
- When was the last time you did something that scared you?
- What kinds of things make you happy?
- What makes you laugh?
- When was the last time you cried?
- What do you do to relax?
- What do you do for fun?
- Is your current social circle influencing you positively or negatively? How so?
- Who is your best friend?
- How would your best friend describe you?
- When was the last time you felt envious of another person? Why?
- What do you still need to forgive yourself for?

- Who do you still need to forgive?
- What are you holding onto that you need to let go of?
- Can you be alone without feeling lonely? If not, why?
- Where in your life are you settling for less than you want?
- What bad habits do you need to stop?
- What good habits do you need to start?
- How well do you manage the mundane?
- What is one thing you love the most about yourself?
- What have you learned about yourself in the last year?
- What part of yourself are you currently working on?
- What do you think is the point of being in a relationship?
- Are you putting any parts of your life on hold? Why?
- What do you spend the most time thinking about?
- What qualities do you admire in others?
- What was the last book you read? What did you gain from it?
- If you have a day to yourself, how would you spend it?
- What really and truly grosses you out?
- What are some of your biggest pet peeves?
- Are you an extrovert or an introvert?
- Do you have any allergies?
- Do you prefer cats or dogs?
- Do you Uber or do you rent a car?

- Do you typically hire someone or do you try to do something yourself first?

- Do you choose paper or plastic (or bring your own bag) at the grocery store?

- What is one thing you cannot live without?

- What do you do for a living now?

- What do you enjoy most about your job?

- What do you enjoy least about your job?

- What are the achievements in your life you are most proud of?

- Do you see yourself leaving (<u>the state you live in</u>)?

- Would you rather live in a house or in an apartment?

- Would you rather live in the city or in the country?

- What do you see yourself doing five years from now?

- What do you see yourself doing ten years from now?

- What does your ideal retirement look like?

Chapter 9:
Common Dating Pitfalls to Watch Out For

"The right guy is out there. I'm just not gonna go kiss a whole bunch of losers to get to him." Josie Gellar, Never Been Kissed[*]

    As you get to know someone new and things begin to get more serious after the first few dates, there are several key areas to watch out for on your journey of falling in love. As you do begin to fall in love, it is easy to ignore red flags or warning signs. When that happens, these things become really big deals down the road. Additionally, as you begin to fall in love, it is easy to become consumed with the person you are dating. When that happens, you can begin to neglect the things that were important to you before you met. This chapter will walk you through just a few of the dating

---

[*] Sandy, I. & Juvonen, N. (Producers), & Gosnell, R. (Director). (1999). *Never Been Kissed* [Motion Picture].

pitfalls to watch out for with some advice to help to avoid them.
ESTABLISH BOUNDARIES EARLY

Do not wait until the "love" drugs are in full effect before discussing boundaries in your relationship. You might think I am referring to physical boundaries only. The truth is, I am referring to boundaries of all types. Boundaries can be anything from physical to emotional to even relational. Boundaries are essentially what you will or won't allow. You can even think of it as a line in the sand. Establishing boundaries in your relationship early will set you up for a happier, healthier, and more intimate future together. Boundaries should be decided on and established as a couple. However, many boundaries can be ideals and beliefs you might have had in mind before you ever got into a relationship.

Physical Boundaries

One of the first decisions you will make as a couple is how far is too far in the physical intimacy area of your relationship. This is a decision you should both come to mutually, neither one pressuring the other. Tim and I both entered into our relationship with the commitment that we were not going to have sex until we were married. This was a conversation we had within the first couple of hours of chatting online. I was the one who brought it up first and in my mind there was no reason to keep talking if we could not agree on that one issue. Thankfully, we both desired to wait.

In addition to waiting until marriage for sex, I had made the commitment to myself before I met Tim that the next guy I would kiss would be my husband. At 32 years of age, I had never had a first kiss. By this point in my life, I did not see the benefit of kissing someone I had no plans to marry. I figured I had waited this long, so there was no harm in waiting a bit longer for the right person. Thankfully, Tim was amicable to that commitment as well. As a result of this commitment, we did not kiss one another until six weeks into our relationship. By that time, we both knew we were committed to each other and marriage was inevitable, not just a possibility.

While we both had the desire to wait until we were married to have sex that did not automatically mean that it was easy to do. Once we began to kiss and awaken ourselves to the intensity of our passion for one another, putting up physical boundaries became all the more important. When I began to go over to his apartment (which wasn't until about a month into dating him and we weren't kissing yet), we made some initial boundaries. For example, when I was over there, Tim left his bedroom door closed. This was his idea because to him he figured if we couldn't see a bed, then there would be less temptation to use one. Kind of like a kid covering his eyes pretending he is invisible. However, he also wanted me to feel more at ease that he was as committed to waiting as I was.

Another thing I committed to was letting one of my girlfriends know when I would be there. Text messages from my most trusted girlfriends (paired with a special, ominous text tone) became a regular occurrence. They would know when I was alone with Tim and would periodically check in with me while I was there. These texts were simple, but having the extra accountability outside of my relationship with Tim helped me to stay more accountable when I was with him.

Emotional Boundaries

Establishing emotional boundaries at the beginning of a relationship will aid in guarding your heart more than anything else. Part of doing that is keeping the "L word" reserved for later. Saying you love someone you have barely had the chance to get to know is not guarding your heart very well. ***In fact, that is giving*** *your heart away to someone who has not yet earned the right to loan it, let alone own it.* Early in our relationship, and I mean early, Tim said to me, "I wish there was a word in the English language between like and love." He was speaking about his feelings toward me. If my memory serves me right, we had gone on maybe two dates at that point—the first date was our awkward dinner date and our second date was going to church together. We had known each other less than ten days.

I met Tim not too long after my ghosting experience where the guy said he loved me before I was comfortable with it. My heart was fragile and not ready to hear the word love just yet. To clarify his remarks, Tim knew he felt deeper than "like" affection toward me, but not quite love yet. We both knew it was too soon for love. He was saying to me that he felt like this was more than just liking me as a person, but that he was beginning to fall for my heart.

I remember when I first realized I did love Tim. It was after nearly roasting to death at an outdoor mall in July. We had gone on a tour of Kansas City and had lunch. Once we ate, we didn't want the date to be over but weren't at a place in our relationship that I was going to his apartment yet. Instead, we walked around the outdoor mall not too far from his place just long enough that I got a migraine and needed to go home. When he dropped me off at my house, I walked in and all I could think was, "I love that man." Migraine and all. Little did I know that he fell in love with me on the very same day.

Relational Boundaries

It is okay, and even normal, to want to spend a lot of time together when you are first dating. There is so much to learn about one another and of course the love drugs are kicking in. But it is vitally important not to lose yourself in the other person. When Tim and I first started dating, we talked every single day, but we only saw each other on the weekend. Our first four dates were four weeks apart. As you are getting to know someone, give yourself some space to breathe. In doing so, you are giving yourself enough time to self-reflect, pray over all of it, and make wise decisions with your heart. Another aspect of relational boundaries is to keep your friends. Relationships with friends and family change once you are married, but those relationships outside of your marriage are still important. If you are dating someone that gives you a hard time about wanting to see your friends, that should be a red flag. The right person will embrace your friends, not isolate you from them.

I had a friend a long time ago that I was really close to when she was single. When she fell in love and got married, her husband began to create a divide between us. This divide started as they were engaged, but it intensified after they were married. As a result of that, she chose him and I haven't spoken to her since. My perception was that he was threatened by me because he felt I knew her better than he did. The truth is, she needed a friend like me. Even now in my marriage, I need a friend like that. It is important to keep some autonomy out of your relationship. It is important to keep safe friends. You and the person you're dating are not an island unto yourselves. You need to have the support of friends around you and that is true even as you enter into marriage. A combination of joint friendships and individual friendships can be nice as well.

DO NOT STOP GOING TO CHURCH

What I have not yet mentioned is that Tim had moved to Kansas, where I live, for a job just two months before we met. One of the first things he did upon moving was look for a church to attend and belong to. He valued the church community he had come from and knew that church was going to be a built-in community in a new city. When he told me that, it immediately impressed me. In fact, for our second date he suggested I meet him at his church and attend the little festival his church was putting on after service. Church dates are excellent, especially if you attend different churches. It gives each of you the opportunity to see how the other worships. Tim and I ultimately ended up at my church. That decision had more to do with the strong church community I had built. Since Tim was new to town, he was able to slide into that community easier than both of us starting over from scratch. However, there is nothing wrong with starting over somewhere together. The biggest thing to take away from this is this—do not stop going to church just because you are in a relationship. Make time for it and commit to it so that you will continue to do so after marriage.

CARING TOO LITTLE OR TOO MUCH ABOUT WHAT YOUR FAMILY AND FRIENDS SAY

There is a delicate balance with this one. While the opinion of your friends and family is important, it is even more important that you practice discernment. You know better than anyone if the person you are dating is the right person for you. The way you can know that for sure, however, is by keeping your relationship bathed in prayer. Ask God to speak wisdom into your heart and mind both as a couple and individually. This is a great practice for every aspect of your life. Not every friend or family member will like that you are spending more time with someone else. Especially if there is any enmeshment going on and you're creating boundaries with them. In some instances, jealousy can enter in and they can begin to speak to you out of that jealousy. Be mindful of their warnings and take them to prayer.

NEVER—UNDER ANY CIRCUMSTANCES TOLERATE ABUSE

One of the very first conversations Tim and I had was about my feelings toward abuse. I grew up knowing that my grandpa physically and emotionally abused my grandma. I heard story after story about what my grandma went through and what my mom and her siblings witnessed and experienced. I also remember being in the car with my grandma one time when we witnessed a man play-fighting with a woman we assumed was his wife or girlfriend. My grandma whipped her ahead around to the back seat, looked me straight in the eyes and said, "never let a man treat you like that." This, from a woman who was never able to leave her abusive husband for good. I explained to Tim that I would sooner forgive him for having an affair than if he ever even raised his hand to me.

I cannot emphasize enough how damaging abuse can be, but also how sneaky abuse can be. Abuse does not always look like bruises covered up by makeup and big sunglasses. Abuse can also look like extreme control, tone of voice, and disrespect. "He's mean to you because he likes you" is one of the cruelest pieces of misguided wisdom women have ever been handed. Abuse can also look like coercion or forcing someone to do something they don't want to do. **Abusers are not always men.** While when we picture abuse in a relationship, we more often than not see a man abusing a woman, the truth is abuse can be committed by anyone. Women can be abusive towards men and often are. Abuse by women can manifest as manipulation, controlling behaviors, and emasculation. Abuse from women can even include physical abuse, which for a lot of men is difficult to admit is happening. It is a blow to masculinity to admit that a woman is hurting them.

No one should accept abuse—of any kind whatsoever. If you are experiencing physical or sexual abuse and need help, reach out to the **National Domestic Violence Hotline**[13] at **1-800-799-7233** from a public phone or visit thehotline.org from a safe Internet-enabled device.

DATING PITFALL QUESTIONS

What physical boundaries do you need to establish in your relationship?

What emotional boundaries do you need to establish in your relationship?

What relational boundaries do you need to establish in your relationship?

How much prayer time are you committing to your relationship?

Do you pray together as a couple and/or individually?

Do you currently go to church?

Do you attend church by yourself or as a couple? If alone, why doesn't your partner attend with you?

Have any of your friends or family spoken any concerns about your relationship? If so, what has been their concerns?

If concerns have been spoken, what has your response been?

Is there is any merit to their concerns?

Do you know how to identify abuse in a relationship?

If you begin to feel abuse is an issue in your relationship, how do you plan to address it?

Chapter 10:
Digging Deeper as a Couple

"You're not perfect, sport, and let me save you the suspense: this girl you've met, she's not perfect either. But the question is whether or not you're perfect for each other." Sean Maguire, Good Will Hunting[*]

You may have met someone and have gone on a few dates with him or her. Now, it is time to dig deeper. Now is the time to see if the affection you feel right now can be supported for the long term. Part of determining if the person you are dating is the kind of person you should marry is seeing if you want the same things and believe in the same things. Going into a relationship with extremely different plans is a recipe for conflict and frustration. Discussing your beliefs and values, as well as your hopes for the future, is

---

[*] Bender, L. (Producer), & Van Sant, G. (Director). (1997). *Good Will Hunting* [Motion Picture].

something that should be done early on. Not only that, it is also a time to dig deeper into your own personal stories. This requires getting vulnerable with each other about the things in your past that you might not be the most proud of. When you plan to marry someone, there should be no secrets between you. This chapter is designed to help you and the person you are dating to navigate some important conversations, even some difficult conversations, but necessary conversations all the same.

THE SWORD OF TRUTH, NOT THE SORT OF TRUTH

Scripture is called the sword of truth because it is piercing. That too is the kind of truth that needs to be spoken when you are dating with the purpose of marriage in mind—the piercing kind. I want to strongly caution you to avoid the spin zone when you are discussing important topics with the person you are dating. For example, consider if you are being totally honest about your dating history. I don't expect you to remember the kid who asked you out for one day in the fourth grade. But is there anyone you may have dated that you have not told them about? Even if the person you dated was not serious, why are you choosing to omit them?

When we went over our respective dating and relationship histories, Tim left a couple of women off the list. In fact, two of these women he invited to our wedding. These were women he had known from high school or from his old church, went on a couple of dates with them, but had ultimately just became friends. I did not know that he went on dates with them until after we were already married. Honestly, it was not a big deal. He invited them to our wedding as friends he knew from high school or church. He felt the couple of dates he had gone on with these women were inconsequential because he was never in love with them. But learning this was not inconsequential to me since I had listed out every single inconsequential date I had ever been on to him long before we got married, or even engaged. *So define the terms!* By now you should probably already know if the person you are dating has previously been married, has kids, etc. But you need decide when you are going through dating and relationship history what details are important to you: sexual history, love history, date history, ... for some, even previous marriage history. Once you define those terms together, be honest with one another about them and do not leave anything out. Truth always has a way of being found out. It is just so much easier to be honest up front.

GET COMFORTABLE WITH GETTING UNCOMFORTABLE

The easy thing to do is to keep good face in front of the person you are dating. You want them to like you. Because you feel like things are going well, you may want to stay in the nice bubble—safe and comfortable—free of the ickiness that can come from getting vulnerable. However, there is not a more vulnerable relationship on the planet than the one between a husband and a wife. So if you are truly interested in getting married, specifically to the person you are dating right now, you need to get comfortable with being uncomfortable. In marriage, you are naked before each other, fully exposed, both literally and figuratively. That vulnerability—being okay with another person seeing you fully exposed—starts in the dating relationship. Not the actual naked part (hopefully you are choosing to remain abstinent in your relationship), but the emotionally naked part, is a big part of building intimacy early.

People often confuse the terms *intimacy* and *sex*. Intimacy is not sex and sex is not intimacy. These terms are also not mutually exclusive. Intimacy is what happens when you are truly safe and feel truly safe with another person. The truth of the matter is, you can have sex with someone and not feel totally safe with that person. You can have sex with someone without the closeness of intimacy. Intimacy is complete closeness and complete openness. Intimacy is knowing that the other person is going to love you, protect you, and accept you.

Part of the closeness and openness of intimacy includes revealing things about yourself that you may be embarrassed about or even have some shame about. Perhaps there are things in your past that you would prefer to keep there and not dig back up. I get that—I have lived that. However, your past has an unavoidable way of shaping who you are. By not disclosing your past to a potential spouse, they are denied a full picture of who you are and how you became you. Once Tim and I knew that we were heading towards a committed relationship with one another, we felt the need to disclose more pieces of our past to one another. For me, it was my history with pornography. As an adolescent, I struggled with pornography addiction as I struggled with unresolved emotional abandonment as a child. Yep, you read that right. I was once a *woman* who struggled with watching pornography. While I had experienced recovery and wholeness from this struggle a long time ago, I always wondered if I would meet a man who would even understand my past, let alone accept it. Guess what? The right person will accept the sins and scars of your past and love the person you are now.

Tim had a history of his own. He is one of the smartest people I know (I mean, near genius level) but due to a severe anxiety disorder paired with depression as a teenager, he dropped out of high school during his senior year. He later earned his GED and enrolled in college—but it was not easy. It took him nearly eight years to graduate with his undergraduate degree. At the time

Tim met me, I was earning my master's degree, so it seemed on paper I had a lot of success. He also came from a family where higher education was greatly valued, so he had some insecurity about explaining why it took someone clearly as smart as he was eight years to graduate. What he did not know at the time, however, I was the only one in my immediate family to graduate with a four-year degree, let alone continue on to graduate school. Completing both with highest honors. He also didn't know that I had gone back to school at the age of 27 after flunking out of community college at 19 with a GPA of 1.7. I had no room to judge him, nor would I. Again, the right person can look beyond the past and see the person you have become in the present. In fact, knowing what I know about Tim's past, I admired all the more the way he fought his way back to achieve his success. A lot of people in his same position would not have.

MARRIAGE AND FAMILY DYNAMICS

Some of the most important conversations that will take place as a couple are the ones about marriage and family dynamics. These are the conversations all about what it means to be husband and wife, what parenting will look like, and so much more. In many ways, these are the conversations that can make or break a relationship. I could not even begin to provide enough examples of all the questions you should be considering at the end of this chapter. That would take many, many more pages. However, I will share just a couple of them. Early in our conversations, Tim and I discussed traditional gender roles in marriage and whether or not we would celebrate them. Traditional gender roles are pretty much what you would expect: the breadwinning husband, the stay at home wife and mother, husband doing the yard work, the wife doing the household work, etc. I do not personally know anyone who adheres to all of these specific gender roles. Tim and I do not either. Tim and I did discuss them and truthfully, I was more traditional about our roles than he was. It was important to me to that Tim took a leadership role in our home—but as I will discuss in the engagement section—a true biblical marriage is a partnership.

Another conversation we had was about holidays and how we would choose to celebrate them. I grew up a little nontraditional: no believing in Santa Claus, no believing in the Easter Bunny, and I didn't even get to go trick or treating. Santa (with the elves, etc.) was a fictional character, the Easter bunny was a creepy, egg-laying rabbit (rabbits don't lay eggs!), and we went to church harvest parties on Halloween instead of going door to door. As I was growing up, I thought I was missing out on something. When I arrived at adulthood, I began to embrace it and wished to approach some of these holiday traditions in the same way. I wasn't sure I would find a husband who also didn't celebrate Santa Claus and the rest. Or who wouldn't think I was bah humbug for *not* doing Elf on a Shelf. Thankfully, Tim feels the same way I do about these holiday traditions. It took having a conversation about it in order to know for sure. Sharing your traditions and how you celebrate them is a good way of beginning to picture how you would do these things together as a couple and as a family. You can also begin to talk about what new traditions you would like to start doing together.

Have you discussed together about whether or not you see children in your future? Tim and I both knew we wanted kids. The only real conversation was when we would start trying and how many would we have before we felt our family was complete. All of these conversations are unique for each couple. Each couple is different and the only requirement is that you agree about what you decide.

FINANCIAL ISSUES

Another difficult conversation that has to take place is one about finances. While this is definitely a marriage dynamics discussion, it deserves a section all of its own. The discussion about finances has to happen before marriage because finances are one the most fought about issues in marriage. There are many aspects of finances that should be discussed: from credit scores, to income/debt ratios, to money management. My student loan debt was (and still is) a sore spot for me. Between my undergrad and graduate degrees both earned at a private, online university, I had racked up quite a bit of debt. I went into my schooling with a husband nowhere near in the picture. I never imagined I would meet Tim and bring a giant pile of debt into a marriage so soon. I honestly thought I would graduate, have a couple of years of paying it down working as a counselor, and maybe, just maybe, I would marry someone before I turned 40. Instead, I met Tim smack in the middle of my graduate program and had to confess to him that I would graduate with tens of thousands of dollars in student loan debt. It felt like some backwards version of a dowry.

Once we were engaged, we decided to merge our finances together into one bank account, which also included a mutual decision to stop using our credit cards in order to begin paying them down and not accumulate more. I am not saying our way was the right way, but merging our finances together meant total disclosure on spending habits and income. It also meant that we could have conversations about future financial planning including buying a house, paying down credit card and student loan debt, and deciding which of us would handle paying bills. This is something you both can decide to do in pieces and parts of, but from my experience, it is easier for one person to handle it. It is important to say however, that whoever is managing it, doesn't make the other person feel like they don't have a say in how things are spent.

DIGGING DEEPER AS A COUPLE

The next several pages hold an exhaustive list of questions to help you dig deeper into important conversations together.

Before you begin to have these conversations, remember what I said about the *sword of truth* vs. the *sort of truth*. These conversations are intended to be piercing and to the point. These conversations are designed to push away all of the fake niceness to open yourselves up to the closeness of true intimacy with a potential spouse.

Do not build your relationship on a foundation that is doomed to collapse. When a relationship starts out with a lie (big, small, or even just an omission of facts), the relationship is built on a weak foundation. For a while, a weak foundation does not seem to show any problems on the surface. Over time, a home's weak foundation can cause cracks in the walls, damage the flooring, and doors and windows can stop opening or closing properly. A weak foundation simply cannot support a strong, healthy relationship just as one cannot support a house. Over time, just like a house, the cracks in your relationship will get deeper and the damage may be a tremendous cost.

Not only do lies put an emotional distance between yourself and the person you will potentially marry, but they are also incredibly difficult to maintain overtime. Lies usually require more lies to keep the first one going. The truth about lies though, is they will almost always be found out and will cause the relationship to crumble from lack of trust, feelings of betrayal, and seeds of insecurity. It is also worth mentioning that if you are uncomfortable asking or answering any of these questions, you may need to check your reason why. You should also check your motivation for even being in the relationship you are in right now. If you are serious about navigating the kinds of conversations that are necessary for determining if marriage is possible with this person, this questionnaire is where those conversations start.

I would also like to encourage you to pray together as you begin these conversations. Ask the Holy Spirit to lead your conversations, to reveal truth about each other, and to protect your relationship as you seek wisdom about a future together.

Personal Values & Beliefs Conversations

How would you describe your faith? Do you regularly go to church? Regularly pray? Regularly read or study the bible?

Can you identify a time that God answered your prayers?

How will married life be different than your single life?

What is your belief about alcohol consumption? Why?

Do you now or have you ever had a problem with drugs or alcohol?

What is your belief about gay marriage? Why?

What is your belief about abortion? Why?

Have you ever had an abortion or been with anyone who has?

What is your belief about traditional gender roles? Why?

What is your belief about divorce? Why?

What is your belief about mental health counseling? Why?

What is your belief about treating mental health issues with medication? Why?

Do you now or have you ever had a struggle with mental health issues?

What is your belief about modern medical treatment? Why?

What is your belief about holistic medical treatment? Why?

What is your belief about vaccinations, including flu shots? Why?

What is your belief about spanking children? Why?

What is your belief about gambling?

Do you or have you ever had an issue with compulsive gambling?

What is your relationship with money?

Have you ever been issued a speeding ticket?

Have you ever been arrested? Why?

Have you ever committed a crime? What happened?

How would you classify your political affiliation?

How informed are you about politics and current events?

Who did you vote for in the last presidential election? Why?

Dating and/or Marital History

Have you ever been married before? If so, why did the marriage(s) end? What do you need to disclose about this relationship?

Do you have kids from a previous relationship? What is the custody agreement? How will these kids be welcomed into your new relationship?

What does your dating history look like?

How many casual relationships have you been in?

How many serious relationships have you been in?

Have you ever kissed in previous relationships?

Have you ever been sexually active in previous relationships? If so, when did you lose your virginity?

Are you committed to abstinence as a couple today?

Is there anything else about your relationship history you need to share?

Marriage and Family Dynamics Conversations

What aspects of your parents' marriage(s) would you want to emulate?

What aspects of your parents' marriage(s) would you try to avoid?

What did arguments look like growing up in your household?

What tasks did your dad take responsibility for and which did your mom do?

Would you embrace traditional gender roles in your marriage?

What adjustments to traditional gender roles would you make?

Who was the breadwinner among your parents?

Does it matter to you which spouse makes more money? Why?

Do you want to have kids? If so, how soon after marriage do you want to start trying?

How do you feel about birth control as a couple? Will you research the best method as a couple?

Would you ever consider adoption to have a child? Why?

Would you ever consider fostering children in your home? Why?

Would you ever consider IVF or other medical intervention to have a child? Why?

What are the most important values parents can teach their children?

Are there any holidays or specific traditions that you hope your spouse will want to celebrate as a family? Why?

Are there any holidays that you do not want to celebrate as a family? Why?

How would you discipline a misbehaving child?

What are some house rules you would implement?

What relationships in your life inspire you? What is it about their relationships that inspires you?

Would you ever consider divorce? If so, what would be the grounds that you would be willing to divorce over?

If you and your spouse got into a hard spot in your relationship, would you be willing to seek counseling together?

How do you feel about your spouse having friends of the opposite sex? Will you stay in contact with previous boyfriends or girlfriends?

Do you own pets? What kind(s)? Will they live inside or outside?

Financial Conversations

How did you see your parents handle finances growing up?

Do you consider yourself more of a saver or more of a spender?

What is your credit score today? Do you have any derogatory marks on it such as late payments, hard inquiries, etc.?

Disclose your personal debt: how much you have, what kind (credit, loans, mortgages, etc.), and how you came to accumulate it.

How do you want to handle finances as a couple? For example, joint checking vs. separate accounts. *The why is important with this one.*

Will you stick to a budget as a couple? Will you work together on what the budget looks like?

Who will handle paying bills and manage the budget?

What types of purchases will you and your spouse talk about beforehand? Will there be a spending limit your spouse can spend before a discussion is required?

Section Three:
ENGAGED

Chapter 11:
The Natural Next Step

"I don't want to be someone that anyone settles for. Marriage is hard enough without bringing such low expectations into it, isn't it?"
Walter, Sleepless in Seattle[*]

My hope for you as you begin this section is for engagement to feel like a natural next step for you. By this point, you should pretty know much everything you absolutely need to know about the person you are dating and visa versa: history, beliefs, values, and if these compliment one another. Whether you are just beginning to think about engagement or already have your wedding date picked out, this section is designed to help you and your partner explore what marriage is going to look like for you

---

[*] Foster, G. (Producer), & Ephron, N. (Director). (1993). *Sleepless in Seattle* [Motion Picture].

together. The conversations to have now pertain to planning your future.

You may be reading this while you are still single or in the early part of dating. Good for you either way. It is never too early to gain better understanding of what marriage is all about.

Engagement is an exciting time. Engagement means you have made the decision to be in this relationship for the long term—as in forever. Getting married is a step that should never be taken lightly. Specifically, what it really means to commit. This section could be seen as a bit of a pre-marital or pre-engagement crash course. If you have followed this book well, there should not be a whole lot left that has been unasked or unsaid. You should be going into this with a whole lot of clarity about who and what you are committing to. That does not mean there aren't some conversations still to be had. Up until now the conversations have been about each other and if this dating relationship is heading toward marriage. Now that you know marriage is happening, this section will help facilitate additional conversations as you prepare to say, "I do."

ENGAGEMENT SHOULDN'T REALLY BE A QUESTION

In a recent Netflix special, comedienne Amy Schumer discussed her own engagement by joking about how most engagements are portrayed in movies and television shows. Specifically, how it always seems like the women are shocked by the proposal. As if surprised that the person they had been dating for so long even liked them. It is a hilarious bit because it is absolutely true. I have never once seen a movie or television proposal that wasn't a surprise. It is not just in movies and television shows that these grand gestures and shocking proposals

---

· Shumer, A. (Director). (2019). *Amy Shumer: Growing* {Television Special]. Netflix.

take place. Engagements have become such elaborate ordeals, when in reality engagements should not be that big of a surprise. I guess it shouldn't be surprising when even high school homecoming proposals (or even "promposals") have become elaborate surprises.

For Tim and I, we talked about *when* we would get engaged, not *if*. In fact, we fell to pressures of social norms a bit about how long we should wait to become engaged. How soon would people think was too soon to become engaged? That is how sure we were. We designed my ring at the jewelry store together weeks before we actually became engaged. The only real unknown about our engagement was the exact day he would finally put the ring on my hand. There just wasn't a question as to whether I would marry him. It might not seem romantic or special, however it is incredibly romantic and special to know that you have a commitment to someone that is not contingent on an elaborate display or a question to be answered.

Asking if someone will marry you should not be much of a question at all. It should be known. There is a saying, *"do not ask a question you don't know the answer to."* Deciding to get married is one of those questions. That is not to say surprise proposals are bad. Of course if that is how you want to celebrate your commitment to one another, by all means: plan the flash mob, jump out of the airplane, or hide the ring in some cake. Send me the pictures and I will celebrate with you. The point is, don't get engaged and *then* figure things out. Don't get engaged and *then* talk about your future. Don't get engaged if it doesn't feel like the natural next step. Part of the whole dating done right thing is dating knowing that marriage is where you are headed. Imagine instead of asking, "will you marry me?" you both just said, "let's do this thing."

LEAVING AND CLEAVING

When you get into a relationship, there is a funny change that occurs. On a ministry planning trip shortly after meeting Tim, I texted him from the plane as soon as I landed before telling anyone else. At the time, I was still living with my parents because I had started a nonprofit around the same time I decided to go back to college. I didn't have much money, so living with my parents was a blessing and a necessity. My parents were supportive of my goals so they allowed me to live with them as I pursued my calling and completed my education. As a result, I had a courteous and accountable relationship with them. In part, this meant letting them know when I arrived safely on trips so they did not have to worry about me. On this particular trip, however, it was not until six or seven hours after I landed that I remembered I needed to let my parents know I had made it. It was a strange realization that I was beginning to become accountable to Tim instead of my parents.

This brings up another point. Asking a father for his daughter's hand in marriage should be symbolic at most. We do not live in a society where a father has more say over his adult daughter's life than she does (*I am looking at you, Jim Bob Duggar*). Tim asked my dad for his blessing only because I knew my dad would get a kick out of it. Unfortunately, Tim couldn't find a good time to do it when I wasn't around. Instead, one afternoon, he just sent my dad a text message. That's right, my husband asked for my dad's blessing to marry me in a text message. It was so perfect though. My dad's response was nothing more than, "100% yes."

In some ways, my dad was more ready for me to get married and move out than my mom. My mom has said that she was spoiled to have me around as long as she did. While she was over the moon that I fell in love and was getting married, she struggled with losing me. Establishing boundaries with our parents is necessary, though it is also important to have grace during the transition. I didn't do this perfectly. I can see where I got married and disappeared for a while. While you are supposed to leave and cleave after marriage, remember that your parents, friends, loved ones, etc. are all transitioning right along with you. Call your mom! (and your best friend too).

MAKE SOME PLANS NOW

Planning the wedding is one thing, but the plans you make for yourselves as a couple for right after actually needs more consideration. The wedding can be all consuming, so planning ahead is going to set you up for success. You don't have to plan out the next 60 years before you get married—however, at least the first year is going to be helpful. One thing to decide early on is where you will live, assuming you remain abstinent and don't live together before marriage (preferred!). If you are both living outside of your parents' homes now, will one move in with the other or will you start fresh? Will you begin in an apartment or try to purchase a house before the wedding? There is no right way to go about it but it takes planning to figure out what will work best for you.

Tim and I knew that we wanted to buy a house though it wasn't feasible before we got married. We decided together that we would move into an apartment and buy a house at the end of a one-year lease. We ended up spending the first six months of our marriage in an apartment from hell. We picked this particular apartment because we wanted to save money to better set us up for purchasing a house. It was several hundred dollars a month cheaper than his apartment and had two bedrooms instead of one so I could have an office. Instead of saving money, we ended up spending hundreds of dollars more than had we chosen the nice apartments across the street.

Nearly all of the extra cost came from exorbitant electricity bills due to outdated appliances. The A/C went out in the middle of the summer just a month into living there. The floor slanted so badly that we often tripped walking to the kitchen. We didn't even use the heat and settled for one space heater for the entire apartment. The stairs to our third floor apartment collapsed. I'd look out our living room window to see nothing but a mountain of trash piling out of the top of the broken compactor. I could go on and on. We really do feel like we paid our dues with that place—the right of passage that every married couple goes through. It ultimately ended with us breaking our lease six months in and buying a house much earlier than we planned.

Another planning conversation to have is about kids. Tim and I had planned to start trying for kids a year into our marriage. I am a bit older so I knew my clock was ticking faster than others. However, when one year came, we felt it was better to wait a little while longer. I had just graduated with my masters and desired some extra time to build my private practice. We had also just moved into our house five months earlier. So you can discuss your plans but plans can change too. **Things don't always work out the way you plan them, so remember to be flexible!**

THE FIRST YEAR OF MARRIAGE

Our first year of marriage was a whirlwind for us—full of life events that could send many couples into a tailspin:
- We lived in the terrible first apartment.
- We broke the lease at that apartment and bought a house earlier than we planned.

- Due to extreme stress and burnout, Tim requested a transfer to a new team at work but it took five months for it to finalize.
- We had to replace a major appliance that broke the first month in our house that wasn't covered by our home warranty.
- We suffered a miscarriage from an unplanned pregnancy.
- I started a required internship for my graduate program and wasn't making much money.
- I graduated from my graduate program.
- We paid off my car only to need to put nearly $1,000 into it in repairs and maintenance.
- Our basement nearly flooded due to undisclosed drainage issues at our house and spent months trying to come up with a solution.

Yes, that was all in the first year.

EVERYONE SAYS THE FIRST YEAR OF MARRIAGE IS THE HARDEST, BUT HERE IS WHAT *DATING DONE RIGHT* DOES:

We know each other intimately. We know each other better than we possibly know ourselves at times. I know what his facial expressions mean. I know what his tones of voice mean. I know what is going on in his life at all times because we communicate. The same is true for me. We share our feelings without shame. We share our concerns without fear. We share our ideas without judgment. When Tim has a meltdown about everything that needs worked on at our house, I am able to remind him that nothing is worse than that first apartment. When I have meltdown about finances because I feel guilty pursuing self-employment when I have a pile of student loan debt, he reminds me that God called me to this work and He will provide. When we go through something like the loss of a pregnancy, we can comfort each other in our grief. We have always said that in our relationship it is "team us" (plus God) and everyone and everything comes after that. When you remember that you aren't in competition with your spouse and that you're playing for the same team, getting through the hard stuff doesn't feel so hard. You have a partner through all of it. That is how you get through the first year—it is also how you get through year 60 too.

LEARN TO FIGHT WELL

I am happy to say that Tim and I have not had a lot of fights, and the ones we have had have been able to be navigated pretty well. Our biggest fight to date was while we were still engaged so it is a good example for dating/engaged couples. While we did not live together before marriage, once we were engaged, we began to spend most evenings together. At this point in our relationship, we had also already joined our bank accounts together so I was starting to do the budgeting for groceries, bills, etc. I would go over to his apartment after he got off work to make dinner and started doing his grocery shopping so that I knew what he had in this apartment for me to cook. I had shared with him that it annoyed me that he did not clip chip bags closed because they would become stale. I bought some chip clips to use for this very purpose.

One evening, I had planned to make tacos because I knew I had the fixings for it at his apartment including a big bag of tortilla chips. I wanted an easy dinner because I was tired and there are not many dinners easier than tacos. When I arrived at the apartment, I found an opened bag of tortilla chips sitting on the counter. Turned out he helped himself to the tortilla chips when he came home for lunch that day. Instead of using a chip clip and putting them away, he left them out open on the counter to get stale. *Again.* I was so angry because he had a clip (we had intentionally bought some), but he did not use it. I mean, I was furious! How could he be so inconsiderate!? He was so shocked by how upset I was over a $3 bag of chips that he began to dig deeper. Turns out, it was not about the chip clip at all. I was upset about another situation going on in my life where I felt like someone wasn't being considerate of my feelings. When I found the open bag of chips, it was easier to take out my frustration on Tim rather than to deal with what was really upsetting me. Was it okay that he left the bag of chips out to get stale? No. However, it did not merit my irrational response.

That one conflict has coined the phrase in our marriage: *it is never about the chip clip.* This one conflict taught us how to fight well by identifying the root of the issue. Just like when I thought Tim was *mansplaining*—I was mad about my dad, not at him. There will be times when fights are actually about old anger or old wounds that the new situation is bringing up. There will be times when fights are actually about outside circumstances. Unfortunately, we have a way of being the worst to those we are closest to. Learning to fight well by getting to the real issue is going to prevent a lot of unnecessary hurt along the way.

ENGAGEMENT AND FIRST YEAR QUESTIONS

Are you currently engaged? If not, when do you plan to become engaged?

Who were you accountable to in your life before you met each other?

Where have you seen yourselves growing more accountable to each other than to others?

What are your current living situations?

Where do you plan to live after you get married?

Are there any compromises that need to be made regarding where you will live? (i.e. selling a house, breaking a lease, etc.)

Thinking about your future, where would you like to be living a year from now? Five years from now?

Do you have plans to purchase a house?

Where do you plan to attend church once you are married?

They say the first year of marriage is the hardest. What aspects of marriage are you currently nervous about? Discuss these with each other.

Think about the disagreements you and your partner have had so far. Can you identify any old wounds or old anger that may have been to blame?

Chapter 12:
Bibbity Bobbity Boo

"When you realize you want to spend the rest of your life with somebody, you want the rest of your life to start as soon as possible."
Harry Burns, When Harry Met Sally*

When Tim and I were in premarital counseling, I joked with Brad, our friend and pastor, that on the day of our wedding he would basically say, *"bibbity bobbity boo"* and a minute later we could run off to one of the church classrooms to have sex. We obviously didn't do that. However, it is a strange thing when you really think about it. One moment, having sex with the one person you love more than anyone else in the world is a sin and literally the next moment it isn't anymore. How could a few vows alter

---

* Reiner, R., Scheinman, A., & Ephron, N. (Producers), & Reiner, R. (Director). (1989). *When Harry Met Sally* [Motion Picture].

something so significant in a relationship as sex? One of the main reasons I advocate for short engagements is because there is a feeling of oneness that begins to take over as you make the decision to wed. Once there is an engagement ring placed on a finger, the urge to be one grows deeper and deeper. Some couples even fall victim to the whole *"we're practically married now that we're engaged"* thing. It is difficult to keep the purity boundaries as clearly defined.

By the time Tim and I were engaged, we were spending time together every single day. The more time we spent together planning our wedding and discussing our future, the more connected we felt. The emotional boundaries we had made earlier in our relationship were blown to smithereens. The physical boundaries we had made earlier in our relationship were even harder to keep. Hugs became tighter. Kisses became more passionate. Hands moved to places I am not proud to admit. We felt married and frankly, it almost felt unfair that we had to wait for a ceremony in order to express the physical affection we wanted to in our relationship. We were like two children waiting for Christmas morning. The more we anticipated it, the more difficult it became to wait. I can almost guarantee this is a tension you too will experience or are currently experiencing. **Engagement ≠ Married**. As ridiculous as it seems at times, it is worth waiting for the bibbity bobbity boo.

LIVE LIFE TOGETHER WITHOUT LIVING TOGETHER

There is so much more to being married than the freedom to have sex. We know this, right? One of the ways to bring you closer as a couple without taking your clothes off, is to begin living life together like you will when you are married. There is a popular notion that you have to live with someone in order to know if you are compatible for marriage. Some will even try to justify the choice to live together before marriage by saying they will live in separate rooms while trying to remain abstinent. I am here to tell you that there is another way to live life together, without risking the boundaries you have set. Tim and I were together one year before we got married. We were engaged after just five months, so we had seven months of engagement tension. While we never lived together, we learned to live life together.

Here is what living life together looked like for us:

Tim and I made spending time together a priority. Since I was living with my parents, spending a lot of time at my house was not a great option because we could not spend time alone together there very easily. We couldn't do the normal, life together stuff. Instead, I drove to his apartment every weekday evening, and again on Saturday and Sunday. Granted, this was not something I did right away in our relationship. It was not until nearly a month into dating that I first went over to his apartment. As previously stated, we had put boundaries on our relationship from the start. Once I started going over there regularly after engagement, we would cook and eat dinner together, watch *Dancing with the Stars* or a movie, and I would drive home at the end of every evening.

On the weekend, I would drive over in the morning on Saturday and we'd spend the entire day together. On Sundays, Tim would pick me up and we would go to church in the morning, or we would decide to go to evening service after spending the day together. I was in graduate school during the entirety of our pre-marriage relationship (and for the first year of our marriage). Some Saturdays and Sundays consisted of nothing more than me sitting on his couch writing a research paper while whining and crying like a toddler. Tim would do laundry to prepare for the week ahead and clean his apartment.

It was not easy to leave every night. It was also not easy

driving the 12 miles to and from his apartment every single day for months. However, we wanted to live our lives as together as we could while keeping the commitment we had set as a couple for purity. It was worth the extra effort to not compromise the commitment we had made. That is how you live life together without living together. It was not all romance and glamorous. It was real life and that makes it beautiful.

WEDDING NIGHT AND (SEX)PECTATIONS

In my recovery as a porn addict, I had to intentionally go through a reversal of behaviors and thoughts in order to rid my life of the sin and shame of sexual perversion. I went from hypersexual to essentially nonsexual while I was single. I was 19 when I entered into recovery and I was 32 when I met Tim. That was a long time of suppression. Getting married meant that my sexuality was going to be allowed to reawaken. That was in sharp contrast to my recovery story and it took some getting used to. I am not saying suppressing my sexual desires when I was single was a bad thing. It was necessary and it was obedient to God's standard for biblical sexuality. The sharp contrast was how being married meant permission to express my sexuality—this time in the right way.

You don't have to have a sexual addiction history to have this tension. I have heard from others, including the experience had by our premarital pastor, that for a lot of Christians who waited for marriage to have sex, the wedding night can be a bit jarring. Some men have difficulty performing physically. Some women have difficulty relaxing and actually experience pain. The *bibbity bobbity boo* of it all proves to be a bit too much too soon.

HERE ARE A FEW PIECES OF ADVICE FOR THE WEDDING NIGHT THAT MAY HELP:

You can choose to not have sex on their wedding night.

I am not even kidding about this. All of the busyness of the day paired with potential travel, Aunt Ida's lipstick mark still on your face, too much to drink at the reception—what have you—a lot of couples choose to take the pressure off by taking wedding night sex off the table.

Spend the wedding night exploring each other.

Part of being newly married is now you're allowed to explore each other's bodies. Undress in front of each other. Take a shower together. Enjoy the Jacuzzi hot tub in the hotel room. Touch each other. There are all kinds of ways to be sexually intimate that doesn't require intercourse. If all of this exploring leads to sex on the wedding night, great! If not, also, not a big deal.

It will probably not go the way you plan.

Most couples do choose to have sex on their wedding night and that is perfectly fine. We did. It is important that you go into it with realistic expectations. There is so much expectation and anticipation about the wedding night. It may be the grand finale of fireworks for you but it might also be a dud.

Don't judge a lifetime by the first time.

I prayed and prayed that I wouldn't have my period on our wedding night—but I did. I was horrified but it was real life. The next morning, when we tried again, I had a massive sinus headache and we had made plans to meet friends for coffee and lunch with our parents before we left for the honeymoon. Have grace for each other. You have the rest of your lives to figure it out. Don't be like Lane on *Gilmore Girls* and believe that sex is terrible because of one bad first time.

Don't just the first time by a past time.

Maybe you aren't a virgin. Maybe you are, but your partner isn't. In the dating section, you were asked to communicate openly about your sexual history, so there shouldn't be any secrets or surprises here. That doesn't keep insecurity from rearing its ugly head. Communicating about what you may be insecure about regarding sexual history is a conversation for now, not later. It may seem like a double standard, but when a woman is a virgin and a man is not, the dynamic is different. While men can and do have body image issues, women are more prone to having them. Especially if she isn't the first naked woman a man has seen. Reassure each other that your sexual relationship is starting fresh and there's no comparison to be made.

What you should do in this season as you prepare for marriage and the marriage bed is to communicate about what you're feeling, not just suppress the feelings. Talking about what you are nervous about, insecure about, and even excited about can help relieve any negative tensions that may build up in anticipation of the wedding night. Before I met Tim, I never imagined I would ever be comfortable being physically intimate with someone. I struggled with body image issues and communicated those to Tim before we were married. My ability to be comfortable in my own skin speaks more to the conversations we'd had than me magically getting over my issues.

ABUSE AND ASSAULT SURVIVORS

In the United States, 1 in 9 girls and 1 in 53 boys have experienced some form of sexual abuse.[14] I cannot even begin to address this issue in the detail it requires, but I felt it deserved mentioning in this chapter.

Sexual abuse or assault can cause a lot of sexual intimacy issues in marriage. You must learn to openly and honestly communicate about your abuse and/or assault history, your insecurities, and even your fears about sex with your partner. Those who have experienced sexual abuse or assault have a difficult time separating the trauma of past experiences from new sexual experiences, even in the safety of marriage.

It is not enough to simply love someone enough. Any type of sexual touch (or even speaking about sex) can trigger a trauma response in a survivor. Extra measures will need to be taken to ensure your partner feels safe and protected in your sexual relationship. Extreme patience is a critical skill to develop, as well as your understanding of sexual abuse and assault. There is no timeline for healing from these issues.

If you have a history of sexual abuse or assault and you desire to heal, healing is possible. There are many trauma-informed methods of counseling that can be of great help. Additionally, couples may benefit from seeking counseling together in order to establish new, healthy, mutually satisfying ways of relating sexually.[15]

GREAT SEX REQUIRES COMMUNICATION

Being a Christian couple doesn't mean you have to be prudes about sex. In fact, it means the exact opposite. Being a Christian couple means understanding that God created sex and if He created sex, He also created the pleasure that comes with it. Being a Christian couple means acknowledging that sex in the context of marriage creates a deep, intimate connection with each other and with God as the creator. Sex is also incredibly fun—or at least it should be. If God intended for sex to be about procreation and nothing more, He would not have made it so pleasurable. Instead, He created our bodies to respond with all of our senses culminating in the climax of orgasm. While sex is not all about orgasms and pleasure, I once heard someone say that an orgasm is a *right*, not a gift. I tend to agree. They were specifically speaking about women.

There's a reason *"faking it"* has become a punch line in sitcoms and movies. A lot of women just don't get there. Not because they don't want to, but because there just isn't time. Where it takes two minutes for men to reach orgasm, it can take upwards of 20 minutes for women. That is a significant difference! As a result, a lot of women do not even want to have sex because it has never been pleasurable for them. For many Christian women who waited, marriage can become a big let down when it comes to sexual intimacy for lack of orgasm—but there is hope.

Great sex happens when you communicate about what feels good and what doesn't feel good. Great sex comes when you think about the other person and not just what feels good for you. Great sex happens when you take the time to care for your partner, especially the wife. There are many resources available to help couples prepare (and improve) the marriage bed, including tips and tricks for achieving orgasm together. One such resource is a website and blog called, *"To Love, Honor, & Vacuum"* by Sheila Wray Gregoire.[16] Her work is mostly focused on marriages and the marriage bed. She also has many resources for wedding night preparation, including blog posts and books. Her materials come highly recommended by me as I used them as a virgin bride.

BIBBITY BOBBITY BOO QUESTIONS

In what ways can you begin to live life together as a married couple today?

Are you feeling any tension about abstinence and the abrupt 'bibbity bobbity boo' that is to come?

What are you most excited about for the wedding night?

What are you most nervous about for the wedding night?

What body issues or insecurities do you currently have?

What other insecurities are you feeling about yourself, your partner, or sex?

Discuss your (sex)pectations about your wedding night.

Discuss your (sex)pectations for the marriage bed.

> *Everything should be consensual, so it is important to talk about it now! Anything you want to try? Anything you don't want to try?*

Once the honeymoon is over, how many times a week do you think you will have sex once you are married?

> *Fun idea: Answer this question at the same time as your significant other — your answers will probably not be the same so now is an excellent time to adjust your (sex)pectations together!*

Do you and your partner plan to go to pre-marital counseling? If not, why? If so, where will you go for counseling?·

---

* Learn about the Pre-Marital Couples Coaching I offer at my private practice, Living on Purpose, at http://livingonpurposekc.com. Virtual or in-person.

The following chapter is heavy and may challenge your preconceived ideas and beliefs about divorce, abuse, and biblical submission. Proceed with grace and an open mind.

Chapter 13:
Marriage is a Choice

"So it's not gonna be easy. It's going to be really hard; we're gonna have to work at this everyday, but I want to do that because I want you. I want all of you, forever, everyday." Noah Calhoun, The Notebook[*]

Despite how easy society has made divorce, marriage is about so much more than paperwork and name changes. Marriage is about two people choosing to love each other for the rest of their lives. A lot of people confuse the idea of love as being something you feel. Feeling affection towards someone is one thing. Love is a whole other thing. As someone who never dated before, falling in love with Tim was simply the strangest thing I have ever done. The truth is, love is a choice, not a feeling. Marriage is a commitment,

---

[*] Harris, L. & Johnson, M. (Producers), & Cassavetes, N. (Director). (2004). *The Notebook*. [Motion Picture].

not a whim. Marriage is about total commitment. When you *choose* to marry someone, you are *choosing* to love them for better, for worse, for richer, for poorer, in sickness and in health, for as long as you both shall live. Since I am older than Tim, I told him I would commit to 60 years here on earth and then I plan to see him in heaven for the rest. The only reason I put a limit on it is because I have a family history of dementia and I really don't want to be 100 years old when he is only 95. Ugh! In all honesty though, even 60 years doesn't sound like enough time, if you can believe that.

No one should enter into marriage with an escape clause, even one as unavoidable and inevitable as death. The escape clause I really want to discuss here is divorce. For a *dating done right* kind of couple, divorce should not even be a thought. I certainly do not wish to judge anyone who has walked the difficult road of divorce. I cannot begin to know all of the ins and outs of why it occurred. Perhaps you have experienced a divorce yourself. If not, you certainly know someone who has. I understand couples that end up divorced did not enter into marriage with the intent of one day getting divorced. No one *hopes* for that. Divorce is incredibly painful. My hope is to help you to never have to go there. There is a tremendous amount of idealism at the beginning of a marriage relationship. The hope is to get married and stay married. What I do know is that divorces do not occur in a vacuum, and what causes them doesn't either. I have many friends and even some family who never imagined they would end up divorced, and yet they did.

When you understand that love is a choice, you begin to understand that staying married is also a choice. You might hear someone give a reason for divorce as falling out of love with each other, growing apart over time, or not getting along anymore, or even the whole *"irreconcilable differences."* The problem with those reasons is they all come down to choice. A choice was made to not love each other anymore. A choice was made to grow apart. A choice was made to stop getting along. Pastor Andy Stanley[17] says, *"Our greatest moral regrets are always preceded by a series of unwise choices."* This is invariably true of divorce.

A lot happens in a marriage between day one and 60 years down the road. However, preparing yourself for marriage requires talking about the real issues that you may face as a couple—whether you set out for them to happen or not. Discuss what you will do in the event of big, scary possibilities—emotional or physical affairs, illnesses such as cancer, the death of a child, etc. Deciding today that divorce is a no-go zone means committing to see all of those things through together, should they happen. It also means admitting there may come a day when you will need to go to couples counseling (or individual counseling). It may mean seeking the advice of close friends. It may mean renewing your vows—not because you think it is fun but because you need to recommit to what you set out to do at the beginning.

Love is a choice.

Marriage is a choice.

WHEN LOVE IS NOT ENOUGH

There are times when the choice to love and the choice to stay married are not enough. There are times when the choice to divorce is made for us because of abuse and/or abandonment. I would never, ever encourage a spouse to stay when abuse is happening. Let me say it again for the people in the back:

You are never required to stay in an abusive marriage.

One of the greatest atrocities of the Christian church is telling a victimized and traumatized spouse to go home and submit to an abusive spouse. I can't be unbiased about spousal abuse given my family history so I won't even try. As I told Tim when we were dating, I could sooner forgive him for having an affair than I could forgive him for abusing me (or our future kids). Biblically, there are two permissible grounds for divorce: *1) adultery (Matthew 5:32) and 2) abandonment by an unbelieving spouse (1 Corinthians 7:15).*

I absolutely believe that a marriage can be restored after an adultery event has taken place. I have witnessed marriages reconcile and be made stronger. I have even attended a vow renewal for such a couple. It is most definitely not easy, however if both spouses want to seek reconciliation, we should support that at all cost.

There is a misconception that abuse does not qualify as a reason for divorce because it is not directly addressed in scripture. I am sorry, but we have got to do better by abuse victims than that excuse. From my way of thinking, there is no greater abandonment than abuse.

ABUSE IS ABANDONMENT

Abuse can be physical (including sexual—yes, rape can occur in marriage), emotional, or mental. An abusive spouse has abandoned their husband or wife by withholding love, safety, and respect by their actions. An abusive spouse has shown their actions to be fruitless and violates the command to love as Christ loves the church. I cannot personally judge their salvation, but their actions are that of unbelieving spouse (and that's even unfair to unbelievers to say that!). Abuse is also the only circumstance where I am supportive of separation. If abuse has taken place, separation is 100% required until it has been deemed safe for the abusive spouse to return. With that said, I want to believe a marriage *can* be restored after abuse. I just do not know that it should be. At least not without significant help, repentance, and evidence of change.

SUBMISSION IS A TWO-WAY STREET

For a long time now, one word that has gotten a bad reputation in marriage is the word *submission*. For many (especially women), the words *submit* or *submission* have negative connotations with control, abuse, and power. There are many reasons for this, but one of the main reasons is how submission has been taught in the church. Instead of teaching submission as a two-way street, submission is most often taught as only required of a wife. Husband and wife are co-equals and co-heirs in Christ. Just as Jesus submitted to God the Father, both were co-equally God in all aspects but had their own roles to fulfill. God created Eve not as a subservient being, but as a helpmate to Adam. Eve was intentional, perhaps God's most intentional creation.

Marriage is first and foremost a partnership. There will be times when a husband needs to support his wife more. There will be times when a wife needs to support her husband more. One of my favorite lines from Forrest Gump is when Bubba says to Forrest, *"I'm gonna lean up against you, you just lean right back against me. This way, we don't have to sleep with our heads in the mud."*[18] It may sound silly, but *that* is marriage and it is a picture of mutual submission.

As for male leadership, or headship, or however you want to call it, author and speaker Jackie Hill Perry describes submission as, *"When a man leads a woman well, she can have joy in her submission because she knows she is being led to Jesus."*[19] I agree with this statement, however, submission is not about fulfilling a gender role. Submission is an act of absolute trust between husband and wife. Submission is also a two-way street. I choose to submit to Tim because he respects me, supports me, and I know he loves me by his actions toward me. I also know that he prays for wisdom and seeks the will of God for his life and mine. It is safe for me to submit to him. Tim chooses to submit to me as well because he knows I respect him, support him, and love him. He also knows I pray for wisdom and seek the will of God for my life and his.

There will be times when I receive greater clarity from God on an issue than he does. There will be times when he does. There will be times we will need to table an issue and come back to it when we both have more clarity. There will also be times when we won't agree on an issue at all. We have agreed together that when those times come, it is his responsibility to make the decision for us. He doesn't get to boss me around. Instead, it is his responsibility in our marriage to take charge when we are at an impasse. That is a heavy responsibility and burden that is placed on him and I do not envy it. Unless Tim gives me a reason not to trust him, I have no reason to question that he will lead our family well.

WHEN SUBMISSION IS WRONG

Now, let's talk about when submission is wrong. There are all kinds of ways submission can be abused or misunderstood as simply being obedient to a spouse. **Here are some examples of when submission is actually an abuse of power:**

- When a spouse is abusive (physically, emotionally, mentally, or spiritually)
- When a spouse demands sex or nonconsensual sexual acts—this is sexual abuse or sexual assault in marriage
- When a spouse withholds sex or uses sex as leverage
- When a spouse wants to bring porn or another person into the marriage bed (swinging, open marriage, etc.)
- When a spouse withholds access to money or uses money as leverage
- When a spouse ignores the kids or uses them as leverage
- When a spouse refuses to take on responsibilities at home
- Submission *never* means a spouse has more authority over your life than God.
- Submission *never* means being forced to do something you are uncomfortable doing.
- Submission *never* means being coerced into sinful acts.
- Submission *never* means living in fear of your spouse.
- Submission *never* means responding to your spouse out of fear.
- Submission *never* means blindly following your spouse.
- Submission *never* means simply obeying your spouse.

And I will just say this: If you are worried about being able to submit to the man you're engaged to, you probably shouldn't be marrying him. If you are worried about being able to submit to the woman you're engaged to, you probably shouldn't be marrying her. Your concern about submitting to them says more about your trust in them to lead you well than it does about your beliefs about biblical submission as a whole.

THE SUN WILL RISE AGAIN SO HAVE GRACE

One final thing about submission and disagreements, Ephesians 4:26-27 NLT says, "Don't sin by letting anger control you. Don't let the sun go down while you are still angry, for anger gives a foothold to the devil." Tim and I made a commitment to each other that we would never sleep in separate rooms or separate beds under the same roof. No matter how mad we are at one another, we do not want to give the enemy more room to divide us by banishing one or the other to the couch. At the same time, we also agreed that sleeping on an issue could actually help us approach it with more clarity. There's a saying that nothing good happens after 2:00am. Choosing to stay in the same room means we can pick up our disagreement first thing in the morning when we have both had a chance to rest and restore. While the sun may go down while we are still angry, we are committed to deal with it when the sun rises on us again.

MARRIAGE IS A CHOICE QUESTIONS

What does it mean to you that love is a choice, not a feeling?

How does seeing both love and marriage as a choice impact how you look at the commitment to marry?

What are your preconceived beliefs about divorce in marriage?

In what ways has divorce impacted your life?

What are your preconceived beliefs about abuse in marriage?

In what ways has abuse impacted your life?

What are your preconceived beliefs about submission in marriage?

How has wrongful submission or coercion impacted your life?

Since you began dating each other, have any of your beliefs about divorce, abuse, and submission changed? In what ways?

Do you trust each other enough to submit to one another as equals in your marriage? Can you identify any concerns or hesitations? How can these be resolved?

Conclusion:
Just a Few Final Words

Always be humble and gentle. Be patient with each other, making allowance for each other's faults because of your love. Make every effort to keep yourselves united in the Spirit, binding yourselves together with peace. Ephesians 4:2-4 NLT

There are just a few more things I want to leave you with as I bring to a close this part of my journey with you:

SAFEGUARD YOUR MARRIAGE FROM GROWING APART

There's been a lot of discussion about divorce and it bears one more conversation as it pertains to safeguarding from growing part as a couple. Part of safeguarding your marriage from growing apart is by making divorce unthinkable. You make divorce unthinkable by making your marriage a priority. You make your marriage a priority by making your spouse a priority. You make your spouse a priority by being intentional in every aspect of your relationship. That part takes effort from the both of you.

I wear many hats—counselor, speaker, author, coach, sister, daughter, and friend. However, my first role is being Tim's wife and Tim's first role is being my husband. That is the hierarchy of marriage. Marriage is a hierarchy that begins with God, then our spouse, and then our children. Just as putting your spouse before God is harmful to your relationship with Him, putting your children before your spouse is harmful to the marriage relationship. Even children from a previous relationship come after your spouse. Children need to see the commitment of their parents. They need to see that no matter what happens, mom and dad are good. The best thing you can do for your children is to show them your commitment to each other. In doing so, you create a more unified front becoming even better parents as well. You are also a husband or wife, before you are a son or daughter. In the sequel to *My Big Fat Greek Wedding*, Toula still has her poor husband Ian left out in the cold. It has been 20 years and she still hasn't learned to establish boundaries with her family. She is now preoccupied with caring for her aging parents as a replacement for caring for her now maturing daughter heading off to college. Her aunt finally sits her down to remind her that she was a girlfriend before she became a mother. Or in the case with you, a wife or a husband.

Though we don't always succeed, Tim and I do our best to be intentional about making our relationship a priority, even when we aren't together. My career requires me to be gone more than him: speaking engagements, writing retreats, visiting extended family out of state, etc. Tim may have the occasional overnight work commitment, however, those are few and far between. No matter our schedules, we have never gone a day without speaking. Not one day since the day we met. I don't mean simply chatting over text message. I mean we have talked to each other by phone or in person every day of our relationship. We have heard each other's voices every day of our relationship and that is something we have committed to. I see it as an intentional way of letting each other know that no matter what we have going on, we are husband and wife first. Even if it is a 10-minute phone conversation while I am at a conference, we give each other a moment in each day to connect.

REMEMBER WHERE YOU WERE

Please don't forget what it was like for you when you were single. The best way to do that is to never criticize or belittle your spouse or your marriage in front of your single friends. I can't begin to tell you all of the times I had friends use me as a sounding board for their marriage when I was single. They would tell me that they were jealous of all of my free time. They would complain about their spouse for doing this or that. They would tell me to stay single because marriage is hard.

Please don't do this.

Please don't chip away at the desires the singles in your life have by making a mockery of your own marriage. They want what you have—as imperfect as it may seem at times. Speak to your single friends like you remember how it felt to be them. Speak to them like you remember the loneliness. Speak to them like you remember the longings of your heart to be married. Complaining about your spouse or your marriage to a single friend will only hurt your friend and your relationship with them.

REMEMBER WHERE YOU ARE RIGHT NOW

Please don't forget what it is like for you right now. Right is it probably seems like you will never have marital issues. I promise you, you will. Marriage is one of the most beautiful things God created and the enemy hates it. Giving the enemy any kind of foothold is enough for him to dig in and fester. There doesn't have to be affairs or giant, loud fights for there to be issues. When you have been married a while it is easy to become complacent. It is easy to take advantage of your spouse because dinner is always on the table, or the kids always get picked up from school, or the lawn always gets mowed. When you take the time to let your partner know you appreciate all that they do, it draws you closer and makes discussing the problems in your marriage easier as well. Remembering the small stuff goes a long way to help your spouse feel seen, valued, and loved.

LASTLY, GROW IN YOUR SPIRITUAL INTIMACY TOGETHER

Spiritual intimacy is the idea that as partners, we grow in our spiritual development together. By doing so, we grow closer together through a spiritual bond. The first few months of our marriage were not exactly focused on building our spiritual intimacy. At the beginning of our marriage, Tim and I were both extremely busy with work, school, and paying down debt to purchase a home. Additionally, both of our faith relationships were suffering a bit as a result. When we moved into our house, we made a commitment to begin praying together more because we could tell we were not connecting as well as we could be. Since then, Tim and I have committed to praying together every night, in bed, before one or both of us go to sleep. He almost always goes to sleep before me so it is usually as he is ready to go to bed. Most nights he will lead this prayer time and there are times when I will lead it. We even pray together when we are separated by work, travel, etc. One of us always calls the other to pray. This goes back to the whole, we haven't gone a day without speaking thing—only now, we don't go a day without praying together.

Once Tim and I began praying together daily, it didn't take long to start feeling a shift in the intimacy in our marriage go from physical or emotional to spiritual. Dan Allender says that, "spiritual intimacy provides the context to be able to come back together, to begin to consider what is really dividing us, and provide in many ways a soothing, healing process."[20] While we always pray, it does not always begin with prayer. This time at night has become our time. Everything else in the world gets shut out and it is just the two of us. We almost always begin by talking. We share about how we are feeling, what we are concerned about, or anything the other wants to talk about. We even had long brainstorms about this book in those times. Some of our most fruitful and intimate conversations have taken place during this time as night.

It takes 21 days to form a habit and there is no greater habit to get into than praying with your partner. I leave you with this challenge: Take the next 21 days and commit to praying with each other every day. It doesn't have to be long, drawn out prayers full of scripture and "Christianese" words. Simply take the time to pray together about what is on your hearts. Trust me, at first it feels awkward and for a lot of people praying out loud is a challenge in and of itself. I promise you though that if you make this commitment, you will not regret it.

About the Author

Crystal Renaud Day, MAPC is a pastoral counselor, certified coach, author, and speaker. She holds a Master of Arts in Pastoral Counseling: Life Coaching from Liberty University and many certifications in counseling and coaching specialties from the American Association of Christian Counselors. Crystal owns and operates Living on Purpose Coaching & Pastoral Counseling. Her work has been featured in the New York Times, ABC News, CNN, Christianity Today, The 700 Club, Outreach Magazine, and more. Her books include Dirty Girls Come Clean (2011, Moody Publishers), 90 Days to Wholeness (2014, self-published), and Dating Done Right: Pursuing Relationships on Purpose (2019). Crystal resides in Kansas with her husband Tim.

Learn more on Crystal's website at crystalrenaud.com or connect with her on social media @CrystalRenaud (Facebook, Twitter, and Instagram).

About Living on Purpose

Owned and operated by Crystal Renaud Day, Living on Purpose provides Coaching and Pastoral Counseling services to women, couples, and teen girls on a variety of emotional & relational issues. **Recovery Life Coaching** is specifically designed for women facing pornography, sex, or relationship addiction. With the support of coaching, women facing these addictions. **Life Coaching** helps individuals move from where they are to where they want to be. Life coaching can be useful for those desiring balance, adjusting to change & transitions, and more. **Pastoral counseling** provides guidance, skill, and tools needed to promote psychological and spiritual growth. **Plus pre-marital & marriage coaching, spiritual development, and more.**

· Learn more about Living on Purpose at livingonpurposekc.com or connect with us on social media @LivingPurposeKC (Facebook, Twitter, and Instagram).

Acknowledgements

To Jesus for Your grace, for redeeming my life, and for loving me unconditionally.

To my husband Tim with all my love. Without you, this book doesn't exist—not because you married me, but because you supported me in every step of this journey with your encouragement and wisdom. You're my forever favorite. I love you.

To Jenny for your longtime friendship and sisterhood. Thank you for always making me feel like a part of your family when I was single, and for still being here for the next part of the journey.

To my mom for your faithfulness to pray for me and for my future spouse (we now know as Tim). Your prayers carried me through some very lonely times. To my dad for your blessing.

To my in-laws Gary and Marcey for creating and raising the very best man I know.

To my Aunt Nonnie for your encouragement and support as I brainstormed this book and as I wrote it. I'm looking forward to many more breakfasts together.

To all of the people who supported this book on Kickstarter back in the summer of 2018. Only a year late on arrival, but here it is! Thank you for your generosity, but most of all, for your faith in this book and its message: Darren & Charla Miley, Tim, Anne, & Charlotte Miller, Amy Dmyterko, Brad Mann, Johanna Espada, Anna Hall, John Fort, Arlene Stinson, Keren, Anna, Catherine, Brittany Morales, Chloe-Ann S., Audrey Reed, Katrina Pritchett, Valerie McCarty, Angela Dieckman, Yvonne Rentschler, Krissie VandeNoord, Jamie Williams, and several others who wished to remain anonymous.

To the 124 people who took my survey. Your responses were extremely helpful to create a book that singles wanted and needed. Thank you for sharing with such heart and vulnerability.

Finally, thank you all who took the time to read this book. It is honor to get to share these words with you.

Resources

Dating Done Right Community

The Dating Done Right Community is a place for men and women to connect with others reading Dating Done Right. **Sign up today at datingdonerightbook.com**. Some of the benefits include

- Receive exclusive content and advice from coach and author Crystal Renaud Day
- Discuss your journey through the book—but not your average book club!
- Locate people from your own community.
- While not a dating site—you never know!

Accountability

If you struggle with pornography or want to safeguard your relationship from pornography, Covenant Eyes is a wonderful resource for accountability and filtering options. Try it free for 30 days with promo code COMECLEAN at covenanteyes.com.

Personality Tests

The following are a few suggested personality tests that will help you to better understand the way your personality is wired. You can find free versions of these tests online though the official versions tend to be more extensive and accurate in their results.

- Myers-Briggs
- Love Languages
- Enneagram

More resources are available at livingonpurposekc.com

Notes

1) Fileta, D. K. (September 13, 2017). *Why aren't Christian singles dating?* Retrieved from https://relevantmagazine.com/love-and-money/why-arent-christian-singles-dating
2) Mansplain / ˈmanˌsplān / *verb*: *an explanation of something by a man, typically to a woman, in a manner regarded as condescending or patronizing*
3) Spears, K. (2019, August 27). *The enmeshed family: 14 signs of enmeshment and how to overcome difficult relationship dynamics.* Retrieved from regain.us/advice/general/the-enmeshed-family-14-signs-of-enmeshment-and-how-to-overcome-difficult-relationship-dynamics/
4) Covenant Eyes (2018). *Pornography statistics: 2018 edition.* Retrieved from https://www.covenanteyes.com/pornstats/
5) Harris, J. (2003). *I kissed dating goodbye*, Updated edition. Multnomah Books.
6) Harris, J. (2005). *Boy meets girl: Say hello to courtship*, 5th edition. Multnomah Books.
7) Bote, J. (2019, July 27). *He wrote the Christian case against dating. Now he's splitting from his wife and faith.* Retrieved from https://www.usatoday.com/story/news/nation/2019/07/29/joshua-harris-i-kissed-dating-goodbye-i-am-not-christian/1857934001
8) Institute in Basic Life Principles (n.d.). *How is courtship different than dating?* Retrieved from https://iblp.org/questions/how-courtship-different-dating
9) Courtship / ˈkôrtˌSHip / *noun*: a period during which a couple develop a romantic relationship, especially with a view to marriage.
10) Bowers, A., Stell, M, and Veltz, A. (2019). I prayed for you [Recorded by Matt Stell]. On *Everywhere But On*. Nashville, TN: Arista.
11) Hudson, A. (2018, May 18). *Meghan Markle's pre-royal 'finishing lessons' and an etiquette of equality.* Retrieved from https://thehill.com/opinion/civil-rights/388298-meghan-markles-pre-royal-finishing-lessons-and-an-etiquette-of-equality
12) Brady, T. (2019, October 18). *Meghan reveals intense media spotlight has left her struggling to cope as a mum.* Retrieved from itv.com/news/2019-10-18/meghan-prince-harry-tom-bradby-itv-african-journey-documentary/
13) The National Domestic Violence Hotline. *Is this abuse?* Retrieved from https://www.thehotline.org/is-this-abuse/
14) Rape, Abuse and Incest National Network. (2016). *Statistics.* Retrieved from https://www.rainn.org/statistics
15) Maltz, W. (2001). *The sexual healing journey: A guide for the survivors of sexual abuse.* New York: Quill.
16) http://tolovehonorandvacuum.com
17) Stanley, A. (2014). *Ask it: The question that will revolutionize how you make decisions.* Colorado Springs, CO. Multnomah.
18) Finerman, W., Tisch S., & Starkey, S. (Producers), & Zemeckis, R. (Director). (1994). Forrest Gump [Motion Picture].
19) Perry, J. H. (2017, July 21). Retrieved from https://twitter.com/jackiehillperry/status/888566584213618688.
20) Allender, D. (Producer). (n.d.). LIFC 602, *Marriage Coaching, Week Two: Coaching couples in spiritual intimacy.* [Video]. Lynchburg, VA: Liberty University Online.

Made in the USA
Lexington, KY
15 December 2019